The Sales & Marketing Guide to

Variable Annuities

Gary H. Snouffer, J.D., CLU

NATIONAL
UNDERWRITER®
The Last Word For Over 100 Years

The National Underwriter Co. • 505 Gest Street • Cincinnati, OH 45203-1716

ISBN: 0-87218-208-8

Printed in U. S. A.

ACKNOWLEDGEMENTS

The sales and marketing of variable annuities encompass a great many disciplines within the insurance and investment business. For all of their help, I wish to thank my former colleagues at Union Central Insurance and Investments and its broker/dealer, Carillon Investments, Inc. Their expertise, insights and guidance were of immeasurable value in the writing of this book.

I also wish to thank the National Underwriter editors, especially Darlene K. Chandler, for their assistance in discussing the issues involved and in editing and checking the contents of the various chapters. Such high quality, professional backup provides a writer with considerable confidence.

ABOUT THE AUTHOR

In his nearly forty years in the insurance industry, Gary Snouffer has worked with annuities from both the sales and technical perspectives. While a vice president with a mutual life insurance company, he played an instrumental role in creating and marketing the company's first variable annuity.

Gary began his career as a life insurance agent, spending nearly a decade concentrating on personal financial and business needs sales. As an Assistant Editor for the National Underwriter Company, where he contributed to *The Advanced Sales Reference Service* and the *Agent's Service,* Gary wrote about the sales process and developed training programs.

After leaving National Underwriter, Gary held various home office positions with Union Central Life, eventually becoming a vice president in the Marketing Department. With Union Central, Gary was responsible for the marketing aspects of product development for both life and annuity products as well as advanced underwriting support services and accumulation product marketing. Additionally, he was charged with the development of marketing and business plans.

Also while in the home office, Gary developed and conducted numerous seminars on life insurance and annuity product sales and technical concepts in the areas of business and estate planning. He designed seminars to introduce new products and explain the effective uses of policy illustrations.

Gary received his undergraduate degree from Miami University of Ohio and his law degree from the Salmon P. Chase College of Law. He is a member of the Ohio bar and holds the Chartered Life Underwriter (CLU) designation. Additionally, he holds NASD Series 6 and Series 26 licenses.

Currently a consultant to several businesses, Gary resides in Cincinnati, Ohio.

TABLE OF CONTENTS

1

THE BOOM IN VARIABLE ANNUITY SALES: WHAT'S HAPPENING?

ANNUITY SALES ON THE INCREASE

Annuities, both fixed and variable, have been among the mainstays of the public's saving and investment choices for some years. Although only recently so popular, variable annuities have been around for over 50 years; fixed annuities have been available for far longer. Whether the public prefers fixed annuities or variable annuities at any particular time has had much to do with interest rates and stock and bond prices.

For many years in the 1980's and early 1990's, interest rates being credited to fixed annuities were at or near historic highs. At the same time, the fixed annuity products being developed contained attractive, new features and flexibility not previously available. There were few drawbacks to turning to these annuities, provided that they were being issued by companies with solid financial underpinnings. Here was a relatively easy-to-understand product with high current interest rates, underlying interest guarantees, tax deferral, and results that were easy to track. What could be better? Maybe nothing could have been better, if these conditions had lasted forever.

But, of course, they did not. Market interest rates plummeted in the 1990's, soon followed by credited current rates on fixed annuities. Add to that the fact that fixed interest financial instruments have a more difficult time keeping pace with inflation than those with equity investments, and it is easy to see why sales of fixed annuities slowed during this period.

Variable annuities have become financial products of choice in ever-increasing numbers during the 1990's. According to *The VARDS Report*[1], published by the Variable Annuity Research and Data Service, sales of a whopping $73.9 billion occurred in 1996 (see Figure 1.01). This followed sales totals of $28.5 billion in 1992; $46.6 billion in 1993; $50.2

1

billion in 1994; and $51.4 billion in 1995. To show how much sales have increased, similar reports for prior years were $4.5 billion in 1985; $8.1 billion in 1986; $9.3 billion in 1987; $7.2 billion in 1988; $9.8 billion in 1989; $12 billion in 1990; and $17.3 billion in 1991. Only 1988's total was not higher than the previous year, probably reflecting the stock market experience of late 1987. Total variable annuity assets reached $501 billion at the end of 1996, up 26 percent from the 1995 total of $398 billion.

Figure 1.01

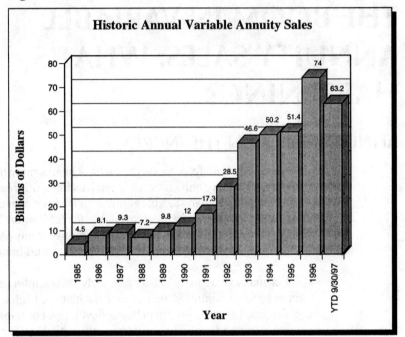

The VARDS Report, Special Report, Year-to-Date (9/30/97) Sales and Asset Survey. Copyright 1997 Financial Planning Resources, Inc. Data is representative of the VARDS universe only. No estimations have been made. Sales are reported on an individual product by product basis. Reproduced by permission.

According to *The VARDS Report* editor's analysis one need look no further than the Standard & Poor's 500 Index for an explanation of these results. The average stock market gain, using that measurement, over the prior two years had been 27.9 percent. For the years 1991-1994, the average gain had been 9 percent, with only 1994 being lower than the year before. Clearly, people are using variable annuities to have their funds invested in stocks and bonds so that they can take part in the very substantial gains that have taken place in recent years. And *The VARDS Report* expects it to continue. Allowing for at least one market decline, the report looks for sales of $85 billion in 1997, $101 billion in 1998, $123 billion in 1999, and $153 billion in the year 2000[2] (see Figure 1.02).

Figure 1.02

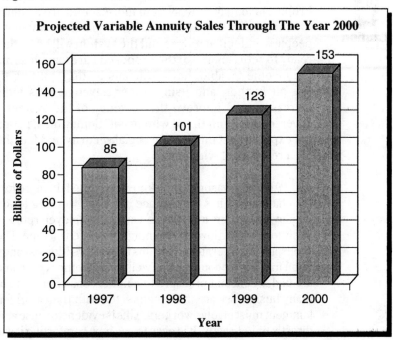

The VARDS Report, Special Report, Year-End (12/31/96) Sales and Asset Survey. Copyright 1997 Financial Planning Resources, Inc. Data is representative of the VARDS universe only. Reproduced by permission.

Variable annuities are a must if one is to offer customers the opportunity to purchase the variety of financial products which often are required to serve their needs. Any number of the customers' financial objectives can be addressed. As we go forward, it will be evident why sales are booming and ownership increasing.

The needs that are addressed when people purchase variable annuities are much in evidence. For the most part, it does not take involved explanations to point them out and discuss them. Sometimes, it takes a certain level of sophistication to understand all of the ramifications and adopt strategies, but the needs themselves are fairly straightforward.

RETIREMENT INCOME IS UP TO THEM

Today, people know it is up to them to provide a substantial amount of their retirement incomes. Much has been written about the baby boomers, those born from 1946 through 1964, because there are so many of them. The oldest baby boomers are now in their 50's, in those years when people begin to "get serious" about retirement. There are many reasons to believe it important to provide for yourself.

Caution

Faith in the solvency of the social security system has eroded. Proposals to make the system more sound are advanced; from time to time, one is implemented. But it is fair to say that a great many people wonder just how sound the system will be by the time they are ready to retire. Some of the proposed cures, such as making more of the income taxable, having means testing, putting the retirement age off further, and using a less advantageous index for benefit increases, may improve the solvency of the system but may have adverse effects on those who use it. Sometimes, people say they do not expect to get much from social security and feel the need to plan for a retirement without it.

Another reason people know they must do more for themselves is the change that has taken place involving working for only one or two employers during a business career. Employer retirement plans are likely to provide a lower percentage of needed income. Then, there is the widespread corporate reductions in workers (downsizing). With competition from other countries as well as from other companies, businesses are under constant pressure to contain costs. Since the largest costs of many businesses are those connected with their workforces, cost containment must involve workers. This is evident to those affected, whether directly or indirectly. It is easy to see how comforting it would be to have one's own source of retirement income. No longer is it possible to assume a substantial employer-provided retirement income as a given in retirement planning.

Some people feel reasonably secure about the future of social security and their employer retirement plans. Nonetheless, many of these people realize the importance of supplementing these sources with retirement income they provide for themselves. As it is said, "You never have too much retirement income." A higher retirement income will afford greater choices of activities, travel destinations, and places to live. It can also create the opportunity to make gifts to family members and charities and, perhaps, even have an effect on the type and quality of health care available.

MAINTAINING PURCHASING POWER

People are concerned about maintaining their purchasing power in the future in light of the effect of inflation on the prices of the goods and services they buy. Many potential annuity buyers have vivid memories of the high inflation days of the late 1970's and early 1980's. Many are reminded of inflation each time they buy, especially with higher priced items such as a car or a major appliance. Home prices in some areas have increased disproportionately. The cost of college has outpaced inflation at a time when a college education is more important than ever for financial success.

People are bombarded, in newspapers, magazines, and on television and radio, with information about costs which affect inflation. Nearly every week one or more leading economic indicators are reported. Every time the Federal Reserve Board meets or its chairman speaks, the impact of anticipated action is assessed as to its effect on markets, interest rates, and other factors. One cannot forget about inflation for very long.

Stocks and bonds as a group are seen as good hedges against inflation. It has been well documented over the years that the S&P 500 Index has increased faster, on average, than the Consumer Price Index (CPI). Twenty-year corporate bonds also have outpaced the CPI, though not by as much. Of course, not all stocks or all corporate bonds will serve to hedge inflation because some will decrease in value. But people recognize that they must be in a position to benefit from the capital appreciation of stocks and of bonds in some cases. They realize that they must put some significant portion of their retirement dollars into financial products which invest in stocks and/or bonds if they are to have the income to cope with future inflation. But that does not necessarily mean that they wish or expect to become adept at selecting individual stocks and bonds.

A MEASURE OF SAFETY

Many people desire a certain measure of safety with respect to the funds they are saving or investing as well as with respect to the earnings that the funds will generate. They understand that fixed-rate products have an interest rate guarantee for some period but that renewal rates will not be known in advance and will depend on current market conditions. In some cases, there is a floor rate below which the renewal rate will not go. Fixed-rate products often have a guarantee of principal. The companies issuing the products are able to offer guarantees because they diversify the investments which underlie those products. They diversify by type of instrument, time period, liquidity, and other factors needed to suit the requirements of the product. It is this diversification that brings safety.

The same principle holds true for financial products which invest in stocks and bonds, except that diversification is a joint effort which includes the buyer. The financial product, e.g., mutual fund or variable annuity separate account will have diversification in keeping with the investment objective of the fund or account. However, the mutual fund or variable annuity buyer must attain this diversification by selecting those funds or accounts which provide the desired level of diversification when considered along with the buyer's other investments and savings.

Planning Tips

As indicated, diversification is the key to safety. Either the buyer has it done by the product issuer or he/she participates in it to a significant extent. When the buyer participates by purchasing products which invest in stocks and bonds, he/she is in a position to enjoy the financial benefits of products which perform better, on average, than those where the product issuer has sole responsibility for diversification.

CONTROL OF INVESTMENT SELECTION

Many people like to exercise a certain degree of control over where their money is invested but they do not necessarily want complete control. They may be willing to put some of their funds in products where the product issuer selects the investments and pays them a promised rate of interest. They may like the idea of having portfolio managers handling certain amounts of the money they are investing. But these people want to retain the ability to direct shifts to other types of investments or to change the mix of the types of investments. They want to feel they are in control to the extent they want to be in control. At times, they will want to be relatively active in the management of their funds, and at other times, they will want to feel able to be relatively inactive with the knowledge that investment matters will proceed satisfactorily without their active intervention. To put it another way, many people like the idea of being able to exercise or not exercise control as they wish; often, these occasions are dictated by the amount of time and attention the people are willing and able to devote.

Beyond that, many people simply do not wish to select individual investments. They have neither the expertise nor the time to acquire the expertise. They may not have the self-confidence to assure peace of mind. In addition, they may not be able to achieve the level of investment diversification needed for the level of safety they would like. The fact that they will be subject to some relatively small fees for professional assistance appears to be a good bargain.

WHEN TO PAY TAXES

When there are opportunities, people like to control when they pay taxes on various types of income and how much they pay. While it is not possible for most employees to do much about when they receive income, they can take some steps such as timing charitable contributions, medical expense payments, and real estate taxes as well as selecting when to take capital gains and losses and sell real property. They also can take advantage of all opportunities they have to participate in tax-qualified retirement plans and to borrow using home equity loans, so that interest is deductible.

Planning Tips

Self-employed persons and professionals have more opportunities because, to a significant extent, they can control or, at least influence, when they receive income and when they pay business expenses. After all customers usually will not pay until you bill them and suppliers will not object to being paid earlier, perhaps at a discount. Magazines and newspapers contain many articles on income tax tactics in the final quarter of each year. People never cease looking for ways to control how much they will pay in a particular year.

LOOKING FOR HELP

Thus far, in examining the reasons behind the ever-increasing popularity of the variable annuity, we have looked at people's recognition that they:

1. need to have considerable responsibility for their retirement income;

2. need to maintain buying power in the face of inflation;

3. want a certain measure of safety obtainable by means of diversification;

4. like the idea of maintaining some control of their investments;

5. may not want to make individual investment selections; and

6. want to have some control over when and how much income tax they pay.

While it is true that people may realize that these are the things they want, many simply do not know "how to get there from here."

Many of these people want and are willing to pay a reasonable amount for help so that they can have a chance to provide adequately for their futures. The help they need can come from qualified sales representatives and financial planners. It also can come from the purchase of financial products that feature professionally-managed portfolios which purchase a large enough number of stocks and/or bonds to achieve a desirable level of diversification. These products are convenient to purchase and offer the flexibility to accommodate any changes needed. As we will see next, variable annuities fall into this category of financial products and can be used to meet many financial needs.

VARIABLE ANNUITIES "HAVE IT ALL"

Convenient to Purchase

One of the factors important to the success of implementing a plan to supplement retirement income is a financial product that can be purchased in convenient amounts, at convenient times, and on a convenient, systematic basis. With most companies, variable annuities may be purchased with low initial and continuing premiums. In most cases, flexible premiums are the rule so that a buyer may elect to make regular payments such as annually, semi-annually, quarterly or monthly. Or the buyer may make periodic or occasional payments according to his/her own schedule.

It often is said that the key to saving and investment success is consistent activity. The effect of compounding interest on earnings and the difficulty of "timing the market" with investments combine to make it difficult to make up for intermittent activity. The company issuing a variable annuity will send a notice to remind the buyer to make another payment. This is much more convenient than expecting the buyer to remember to send a payment or otherwise take the initiative to save or invest.

Of course, reports, which also offer opportunities to put additional money in, are sent with a number of other financial products, but the ease of buying variable annuities, coupled with their other features, makes systematic saving and investing very easy indeed.

Offer a Multitude of Choices To Maintain Buying Power

Building upon an understanding that a financial program almost certainly must invest in stocks and bonds if future buying power is to be maintained in light of inflation, variable annuities have funds available which cover a wide range of investment approaches. Some of these types of funds may be described as:

- growth

- aggressive growth

- growth and income

- corporate bonds

- government bonds

- balanced

- high-yield bonds

- international stocks

- international bonds

- those using indexes such as the S&P or NASDAQ.

Add to this list, which is not a complete list, a guaranteed interest account, and the buyer has a multitude of choices.

Not all variable annuities have all of these funds but, on the other hand, they often have more than one of a particular type. These funds are managed by professionals and a buyer merely allocates how much of his or her payments are going into the funds selected. The buyer usually has no restrictions as to what percentage or amount may be allocated to what account. And he/she can change the allocation or move money from one fund to another as permitted by the variable annuity contract. As a result, the buyer is able to allocate as much or as little as he/she wishes to funds which offer the promise of maintaining future purchasing power. And, he/she can select from among funds which are as aggressive as he/she thinks desirable to accomplish the goals intended.

Name Recognition

Definition

Some of the funds included in many variable annuities are proprietary; that is, they are provided by and managed by the investment managers of the issuer of the variable annuity. Other funds are provided and managed by other financial organizations, many of which have high name recognition in the marketplace. Having available for allocation of payments funds provided by familiar names can be attractive and a source of comfort for many variable annuity buyers. They may associate publicity with presumed good performance. This conclusion may or may not be justified because the favorable publicity may or may not pertain to the particular variable annuity fund, a fact which must be disclosed.

Publicity about the favorable performance of, for example, a mutual fund provided by the same organization as a variable annuity fund cannot be used to promote the variable annuity. That is because the two funds are different, usually have somewhat different objectives, may have different managers, and as a result, cannot be expected to perform in the same way in the future. All of that does not keep prospective annuity buyers from preferring names they have heard of over those they have not. It is important in these cases that a sales representative not allow the impression to remain with the buyer that information other than that pertaining to particular variable annuity funds may be relied on. Performance data on the fund under consideration is available from the issuer or from several independent sources discussed in Chapter 5.

Control of Investment Allocation

Example

Variable annuities make control of the allocation to investment accounts easy. When they make their first purchase, buyers allocate among the various accounts. In many variable annuities, they also have a guaranteed interest account available. As time goes by, they can change the allocation of the payments they make. They also can reallocate current funds among the various accounts as provided by the contract. This means buyers can become more aggressive or less aggressive; they can resort to more money in guaranteed accounts or less money. They can concentrate more on accounts which produce income. They can concentrate more on accounts which hold the expectation of capital appreciation. Then, when the buyers' needs for income become different, they can change the allocations or move money from one account to another.

Naturally, the various accounts perform differently from each other at different times. The result can be that a variable annuity buyer may find that the various accounts are not maintaining the balance among the various accounts he/she intended. The buyer may rebalance the accounts by making transfers among them, subject to contract provisions. In some instances, the buyer can direct that automatic rebalancing be done on a periodic basis. All of these procedures make it possible for the variable annuity buyer to remain in control of the allocation to investment accounts, all without the necessity of selling some investments and buying others with resulting sales charges and tax consequences.

Tax Paying Control

So long as premiums are paid into a variable annuity and no withdrawals are made, income taxes are not incurred by a variable annuity owner; rather, they are deferred until such time as money is withdrawn in some manner. What income tax is payable at the time of withdrawal depends on a number of factors, most notably how the money is withdrawn and how old the annuity owner is at the time of withdrawal. We will examine matters of taxation in other chapters and more completely in Chapter 12, but the general rule is that any money taken out is subject to tax.

Reminder

This means that, as indicated, until money is withdrawn, it is not subject to current income tax. To the extent the buyer controls when withdrawals are made from a variable annuity, he/she controls income taxation with respect to it. Many savings and investment products cause the owner to incur income taxes even though all earnings are left in the product and the purchaser receives no actual income or other earnings. To be sure, the income and earnings serve to increase the value of the other products and any income taxes paid increase the taxpayer's basis for the future, but the purchaser is not in a position to control how much is to be considered distributed and when the taxes are incurred. With variable annuities, the owner is in a better position.

Income Amount and Timing Control

A person buys a variable annuity with the intention that he/she will take income from it at some time in the future. Although he/she may have percentage or amount restrictions for some years or tax consequences, including tax penalties until age 59½, eventually the buyer can take about what is wanted from an annuity. Even during the early years of restrictions, substantial amounts can be withdrawn. This kind of freedom gives the buyer considerable control of the timing of income to be received. And again, these actions can be taken without selling one financial product and buying another. It is all part of the full sequence of events expected in the life of a variable annuity.

There is one more important factor with respect to the amount of income. It is one unique to annuities. An owner may elect to have annuity proceeds paid over a period of years or even for life. The payout can be either a fixed amount or it can be variable. That is, the amount that is paid each time will vary according to the performance of the investments in the account(s) from which it is being withdrawn. The variable payout allows the annuitant to continue his or her participation in equity investments.

Planning Tips

The income is made up of both principal and interest and, for that reason, is a larger amount than would be the case if only interest or earnings were being distributed. When a life income is elected and the annuitant is, for example, in his or her upper sixties or older, the income is considerably higher than interest or earnings alone and it will last as long as the annuitant lives. For lower income annuitants, this can be of major benefit. Still again, this is the same financial product that was being used for other purposes earlier in the owner's life. Material changes need not have been made.

IN THE FOLLOWING CHAPTERS

We will examine all important aspects of variable annuities in the chapters that follow. We will look at markets, including those who want adequate retirement, entrepreneurs and other self-employed persons, those who want to be able to postpone taxes with flexibility, those who need to maximize income that will last forever, and those who need to put to work some large proceeds they have realized, in Chapter 2. Next, in Chapter 3, we will talk about approaching markets, the need for many transactions, target marketing, seminar selling, approaching employers with and without tax-qualified retirement plans, contacts as a regular part of servicing customers, and building your sales story and sales presentation.

Sales Tips

Selling ideas are in Chapter 4. Among these are maintaining buying power, the confidence of having many choices, maintaining and changing the investment mix, getting in and out of guarantees, controlling when you pay income tax, drawing income when you want it, making maximum use of IRAs, including the new ones, dealing with large amounts of money, and long-term gifts to children and grandchildren.

Chapter 5 addresses marketing and sales support topics such as past histories, dollar cost averaging, asset allocation, sales illustrations, rebalancing accounts, and using the prospectus. Variable annuities are registered products and SEC, NASD, state insurance department, and broker/dealer compliance requirement discussions are in Chapter 6.

Product features and characteristics of variable annuities are in Chapter 7. Here we look at both the common and the less common. Charges and fees are considered in Chapter 8, in the context of how variable annuities are priced. Pricing is an important subject when comparing products and the comparison must take together all of the elements available if it is to be accurate. Factors having to do with the distribution of variable annuity products, including the compensation of the various parties, are taken up in Chapter 9. These matters also have a material bearing when making product comparisons. Of course, comparisons also extend to products other than variable annuities. Those other financial products used for saving and investment are discussed in Chapter 10.

Variable annuities have significant uses in business and estate planning as we will see in Chapter 11. A very important one is in tax-qualified retirement plans as well as plans to supplement qualified plans. In addition we will consider gifts to charities and individuals and structured settlements. In Chapter 12, we will conclude with the important taxation and ownership provisions affecting variable annuities. Included are income tax aspects applicable to the accumulation period and to withdrawals, exchanges under Code section 1035, and periodic payments, as well as federal estate and gift tax considerations. Ownership and beneficiary aspects also are covered.

Variable annuities are versatile and exciting financial products to market and sell. They can be a major answer to many customers' financial needs. Understanding them and accurately portraying their benefits and features in the context of customers' financial needs can be rewarding to your customer and to you.

CHAPTER FOOTNOTES

1. "Special Report, Year-End (12/31/96) Sales and Asset Survey", *The Variable Annuity and Research Data Service (VARDS)*, Financial Planning Resources, Inc.

2. *Ibid.*

2

MARKETS FOR VARIABLE ANNUITIES

BUILDING ON MUTUAL FUND AWARENESS

Though the prominence of variable annuities is rather recent, the public has been well aware of mutual funds for a far longer time. The first mutual fund in the United States was established in 1924. The Investment Company Act of 1940 defined and classified investment companies, established minimum capital requirements, and provided for other requirements. The Investment Company Amendments Act of 1970 made refinements. The result has been that mutual funds are among the most highly disclosed and publicized of the financial services industries.

Because so much information is readily available, nearly every issue of financial papers such as *Barron's* or the *Wall Street Journal* and of monthly financial or financial planning magazines have articles on mutual funds. It seems there is always something going on with purchase trends, performance of certain sectors, changes in investment managers, and other news. When editors have nothing else to report, they can always put out a ranking of the top 10 or 25 or 50 funds of a certain type over certain periods of time. And they usually follow that with the bottom rankings in the same category. Since readers seem to like such scorecards, the stories attract attention.

The Investment Company Institute indicates there are some 30 million mutual fund investors. In a recent study[1], it was found that the "typical" mutual fund investor is 44 years old, has $60,000 of income, is married and employed. Overall, 58 percent have at least four years of college and 20 percent have completed graduate school. As would be expected, the number of funds owned increases with income. For those earning approximately $40,000 to $75,000, 12 percent owned seven or more funds while 29 percent owned four to six funds. For those earning $75,000 or more, 22 percent owned seven or more and 30 percent owned four to six funds. These fund ownership numbers are without regard to any funds that employers maintained in their retirement plans. It is pretty easy to conclude that mutual funds have wide recognition, approval and ownership.

The reasons cited for the high acceptance level of mutual funds are diversification, professional money management and liquidity. An investor with virtually any size account can have these advantages. Most individual investors do not have the time, the money, or, in many cases, the desire to select individual securities, diversify widely enough to achieve an acceptable level of safety, and learn and stay abreast of financial, industrial, and worldwide developments that could affect the performance of their investments. And, although mutual funds offer professional money management, individual investors can make their own changes by taking money from one mutual fund and putting it into another.

INSIDE THE VARIABLE ANNUITY WRAPPER

Definition

In most respects, a variable annuity is a package of mutual funds in a unified wrapper, which also may contain a guaranteed account. (As was said earlier and will be discussed in more detail in Chapter 10, the variable accounts in a variable annuity have some differences from mutual funds.)

A variable annuity has some distinct advantages over a collection of mutual funds. First in importance is income tax deferral. While funds are accumulating in a variable annuity, there is no current income tax to be reported. Income tax is paid when money is withdrawn or paid out from the annuity. There is a price for the tax deferral, of course. Unless one of the exceptions (discussed in Chapter 12) applies[2], there is a 10 percent penalty on any taxable distributions prior to age 59½. Further, except for periodic payouts, all taxable interest and earnings must be taken before the previously taxed investment or principal can be withdrawn.[3] Finally, there is one other factor. Some mutual fund distributions are subject to capital gains and losses; all variable annuity distributions receive ordinary income tax treatment.

Planning Tips

The tax deferral wrapper of a variable annuity offers yet another advantage. Funds may be moved from one account to another without the necessity of having to buy and sell shares. This means there need be no tax reporting when money is transferred as is the case with mutual funds.

In addition, a variable annuity has a death benefit. That is, in the event of the death of the annuitant, there is a guaranteed minimum amount which will be paid to a beneficiary. What the minimum is varies (as discussed in Chapter 7), but it will never be less than the amount of money put into the contract. No such guarantees are available with mutual funds.

Another advantage of a variable annuity is the availability of payout options, including those which pay for the life of the annuitant. This enhances the value of the variable annuity as a financial product for retirement considerably.

And, after all, most people are investing for retirement. There may be some shorter range goals, particularly the education of children, but retirement is at or near the top of every list of financial objectives. The biggest group of people interested in saving and investing for retirement is the baby boomers. Born from 1946 through 1964, the baby boomers number some 78 million and they are at or moving into their peak earning years.

CHANGES IN HOUSEHOLDS

According to Census Bureau figures for 1995, the latest year available, the mean income for all households was $44,938. For householders, ages 35-44, the mean was $53,230. For those ages 45-54, the mean figure was $59,636. At ages 55-64, the mean was lower at $50,349. "The current income of baby boom households is substantially greater on an 'income per adult equivalent' basis (similar to a per capita measurement) than that of their parents at the same age ... because they have had fewer children and because baby boom women are more likely to work than were their mothers."[4]

To subdivide household incomes a bit, the Census Bureau figures show that among all households, the upper limit for the third fifth of the 99.627 million households in 1995 was $42,002. The upper limit for the fourth fifth was $65,124, and the lower limit for the top 5 percent was $113,000.

To be sure, the composition of households is undergoing changes. In 1980, Census Bureau figures showed that about 31 percent of households consisted of married couples with children, about 30 percent were married couples without children, and almost 23 percent were people living alone. (Other types of family and non-family households made up the remainder.) By 1995, married couples with children were down to about 25 percent, married couples without children were at about 29 percent, and those living alone had risen to 25 percent. By 2010, it is estimated that married couples with children will make up 20 percent, married couples without children will be up to 32 percent and those living alone will amount to almost 27 percent of households.

This shift will have consequences for the popularity and sales of financial products and services as well as for many other products and services. However, the trend does nothing to minimize the need of people in all types of households to have sufficient income for retirement. If anything, the shift will reduce the ability of many retirees to obtain financial assistance from their still-working children. Many simply will not have children able to help them.

CHANGES IN RETIREMENT INCOME COMPOSITION

According to a report from the Employee Benefit Research Institute (EBRI) and the National Academy on Aging, the average American retiree now receives about 36 percent of retirement income from social security, 25 percent from assets, 18 percent from employer pensions, 12 percent from wages, and 9 percent from other sources.[5] By the time the baby boomer population reaches retirement, these sources will have experienced a number of changes and, thus, the retirement picture will be quite different than it is today.

Social Security

A much publicized change is the one affecting social security. Today, those over age 65 represent 12 percent of the U. S. population; by 2029, when the youngest baby boomer reaches age 65, the over age 65 population will be 20 percent. Today, there are roughly 3.2 workers for each social security beneficiary. It is anticipated that by 2029 there will be just 2.1 workers for each social security beneficiary.[6]

The gravity of the situation is being discussed and there are some proposals being evaluated. One that already has been put in place is a gradual increase in the normal retirement age for social security purposes. That will be all well and good, given the fact that it may be possible, even likely, that baby boomers will be able to work to a later age because of improved health and longevity. One required ingredient in this formula is that valuable and pleasing employment remain available for those in their sixties and beyond. The employment atmosphere today, affecting workers in their late fifties and early sixties, would seem to suggest that not to be an entirely dependable prospect.

Caution

The uncertainty of social security is recognized among the baby boomer population. Sixty-two percent of 35-to-54 year-olds surveyed think social security benefits will be cut in the future. Fifty-four percent do not believe they will receive any social security benefits in retirement.[7] The question is, will people who have reservations about receiving social security save and invest more on that account? The answer may be yes. Studies show that the people who save the most are those with the least confidence in social security.[8]

Employer Retirement Plans

The amount of retirement income to be derived from an employer retirement plan also is changing. First, there has been a shift from defined benefit plans, where coverage of eligible employees is compulsory and the employer made most of the contributions and virtually all of the investment decisions, to defined contribution plans, 401(k) plans and other profit sharing plans.

While more workers are covered today and vesting periods are shorter, employers often are contributing less per employee, and the employer contributions more often are dependent on contributions from employees. Defined contribution plans work fine for young employees but are not as rewarding for older employees. Employees who need to consider retirement needs sometimes pass up opportunities to participate in tax-advantaged plans or do not avail themselves of the opportunity to select the types of investment accounts that may be best for them.

Retirement income from an employer plan can be affected even more when the worker does not remain employed long enough to produce a significant benefit. Because of today's shorter vesting schedules, it is more likely that the worker will qualify for some benefit when he/she retires in the future. But the benefit may not be very large. Further, any period the worker spends working for an employer who does not have a plan, or working as a self-employed person before starting a plan, will not add to it. More and more people are changing employers or going to work for themselves, sometimes voluntarily and sometimes not. There can be many advantages to changing jobs or going into business for one's self under the right conditions, but building a retirement income from an employer plan is not one of them.

Reminder

The significance of one family having benefits from two retirement plans available should be mentioned. As stated above, many baby boomer households will have both parents working and presumably qualifying for employer retirement plans. This may or may not turn out to be the case, of course. One parent or the other may take time out for child rearing; one may work for an employer who does not have employee benefits or be self-employed. And then, there is the fact that divorce can alter all of the plans made beforehand.

These same dual-benefit considerations apply to social security benefits. The retirement benefit paid to the spouse who has not worked continuously probably will be less than it would have been otherwise, but it may be greater than it would have been as only the spouse of a retired worker.

The facts and figures with respect to the impact of changes in employer retirement plans are not as well understood as those having to do with social security. One of the reasons is that employer plans vary a great deal and are not publicized outside the employer company. (Sometimes, they are not well understood inside the company either because they are somewhat complicated or because the employer does not want the information disseminated widely for competitive reasons.) On the other hand social security has a number of political aspects and becomes the subject of many speeches and statements, often quite superficial and providing more heat than light.

One's Own Assets

The third major source of retirement income is one's own assets, for the most part the money an individual has saved and invested. Here there seems to be a significant gulf between expectations and actions. One survey, the sixth annual Phoenix Fiscal Fitness Survey of people between the ages of 30 and 59, earning at least $40,000, found that respondents indicated a need for an annual retirement income of $45,000, which would require $750,000 to be available at 6 percent. Yet, the people estimated they would be able to accumulate as much as $515,000.[9] To provide the $45,000 annual retirement income, either the amount of income produced would be less than needed or the person would have to earn close to 9 percent continuously, a tall order. Interestingly, another finding of this same survey was that 41 percent of respondents are strongly or somewhat uncertain about what to do with their money. A study of baby boomers done for the American Association of Retired Persons found that 87 percent of the respondents said they, "... may not need social security when I retire but want to know it is there in case I do."[10]

Not Saving What Is Needed

According to an EBRI survey, many of today's workers believe they will be able to maintain their current standard of living in retirement, and some think their standard of living will improve. But retirees tell a different story. On average, they believe their lifestyle has declined since they stopped working. While 18 percent say they had a "very comfortable" lifestyle while working, only 13 percent describe their current lifestyle that way. Two in ten retirees say they are "just making ends meet," compared with 16 percent who feel this was the case when they were working. Ten percent of retirees say they are "struggling to get by," compared with 7 percent who say they were struggling before they retired.[11]

Caution

One of the most telling statements has been written by Stanford Economics Professor B. Douglas Bernheim. His calculations, based on an elaborate computer simulation model, as well as on a survey of several thousand households, "... reveal that the average baby boomer is saving at little more than one-third of the rate required to achieve the standard of living enjoyed before retirement. The average boomer must roughly triple his or her rate of saving or face a potentially precipitous decline in standard of living after retirement."[12]

A number of people raise the point that since the parents of the baby boomers have done well financially, millions of dollars will be transferred to them through inheritance and lifetime gifts. But the distribution of wealth is highly skewed. While some boomers will inherit sizable sums, "estimates place the median inheritance in the range of $20,000 to $30,000, even lower if the boomer's parents encounter significant end-of-life expenses."[13] If that range is the median, half of the boomers will receive less. The fact is, it appears that there will be a large wealth transfer in the future, but it will be when the higher earning baby boomers themselves make lifetime gifts or die.

There is a somewhat contrary view on what the savings rate of baby boomers is. According to the Employee Benefit Research Institute, if housing wealth is taken into account, baby boomers are saving at 84 percent of the rate needed to maintain their standard of living in retirement.[14] That is, the larger value of the housing of baby boomers should be considered when looking at their saving rate. Studies claiming that the saving rate is one-third what is needed exclude housing. In order to factor in housing, it is necessary that it be acknowledged that people will be able to turn housing into income by downsizing, borrowing by means of home equity loans, and reverse mortgages, plans where financial institutions would provide income on the security of the eventual sale of the home. Some people will want to factor in these expanded uses of their homes and some will not. Many consider their homes to be at least somewhat sacrosanct and not a part of their retirement income plans.

Planning Tips

It is clear from all of this that baby boomers are ideal prospective customers for variable annuities. Those who are not saving and investing enough now can benefit from the convenience and ease of purchasing variable annuities which are most appropriate for retirement planning because of their long-term and tax-deferred nature. Those who do not know where to put their money can benefit from professional money management, diversification, and the flexibility inherent in being able to make changes and reallocations later. Those who need to have some of their funds in guaranteed accounts can do that. Those whose savings and investment actions eventually fall short of their plans can benefit from the availability of annuity payout options which maximize the income that can be produced from the capital available. It is as if variable annuities were created for people with the characteristics of baby boomers.

THE EISENHOWER GENERATION

Definition

All of the attention paid to baby boomers should not take away from another very deserving group of people, those born between 1930 and 1945. Called by some the "Eisenhower Generation," they were 14 percent of the population in the 1990 census (compared to 13 percent for those older, and 32 percent for baby boomers). They are said to "mix the attitudes of their elderly parents with those of their baby boomer children. They spend freely on grandchildren, new cars and homes, and travel, but are also saving for retirement...Their education levels are much higher, their incomes are a little bit better, and there are more working women."[15] The oldest of these are at or near retirement and the others are in their peak earning years and very actively saving. They have some of the saving and thrift attributes of their parents. Sixty-one percent of pre-retirees who save money are actively saving for retirement, compared to the lower rate of 38 percent for baby boomers.[16]

People in the Eisenhower Generation are described as more interested in enjoying life, self-fulfillment, and self-gratification. "Unlike their parents, they believe that life is for the living and not for saving to give to your children and grandchildren."[17] They have the money to spend on grandchildren and on themselves. They are traveling frequently, often for the first time. They are returning to hobbies they once enjoyed, taking up musical instruments, gardening, woodworking, and painting. All of this means these people have large amounts of discretionary income to devote to saving and investing for retirement and other purposes.

Planning Tips

For the Eisenhower Generation, variable annuities are ideal. Since many already are saving and investing for retirement and most of the others wish they were doing better than they are, there is less need to convince them of the desirability of doing so. The ease of purchase, the value of tax deferral, the benefits of diversification and professional money management, the availability of guaranteed accounts, the efficiency of annuity payout options, all advance their savings and investing goals. Control over withdrawals after retirement which might enable these individuals to do the extra traveling and other spending they want adds to the worth of variable annuities. For those who have already retired, variable annuities offer places for their existing funds which can reduce their worries and concerns and even enhance what they are able to do with the funds they have.

OTHER POPULATION SEGMENTS

The 13 percent of the population already at retirement age also are prospective customers for variable annuities, especially for the distribution of funds they already have accumulated. Some will want to manage their own income stream by making withdrawals from annuities; others will want to avail themselves of the opportunity for annuity payouts, on either a variable or fixed basis. Some will want to continue a relatively active management of the mix of their investments by moving money from one account to another from time to time while other people will enjoy the freedom of not having to manage even to that rather limited extent. And the professional money management and high degree of flexibility and liquidity within the variable annuity contract will appeal to a great many.

Financial writers say that younger workers should not be ignored. They say that many people younger than baby boomers, those referred to as Generation X, are relatively more serious about their financial futures than baby boomers were at their ages. That is because the Generation X group has found well-paid jobs harder to locate and is already aware that providing for the future is largely up to them. Though many of these people are not well paid, the value of time in accumulating assets for the future makes buying variable annuities an effective financial product for their futures. Of course, some Generation X members are doing quite well financially. They are excellent prospective customers for variable annuities when they have begun to think seriously about accumulating for the future, especially eventual retirement.

The children of baby boomers are markets for the future. It is expected that there will be a "new baby boom," somewhat smaller than the recognized one because baby boomers are having fewer children than their parents and many women are having them later in life. However, the next baby boom will grow in size over the next two decades as immigrant children, teenagers, and young adults join its ranks.[18] Though there may be fewer current variable annuity customers among this group, the future looks bright.

Thus far, we have looked at the broad segments of the population, portions of which constitute markets that are or ought to be interested in buying variable annuities. The great majority of these people are wage earners or were wage earners before they retired. Many self-employed persons should also consider variable annuities for retirement saving and investing.

SELF-EMPLOYED: IRA AND SEP

Self-employed individuals may use Individual Retirement Accounts or Annuities (IRA) or Simplified Employee Pensions (SEP) to accumulate for retirement. The contributions to these plans are income tax deductible, and the interest and earnings are tax deferred while they remain inside the plans. Both of these plans have contribution limits, as discussed in more detail in Chapter 11. Some individuals have been self-employed for most of their working lives. Long ago, they decided that working for themselves had many advantages, notwithstanding the disadvantages such as no employer retirement plan or other fringe benefit programs.

In recent years, more and more people have become self-employed who heretofore would not necessarily have chosen that route. This is the result of reductions in the employee force (downsizing) in some companies and of the greater use of part-time and/or temporary employees by many companies. These cost-cutting measures are being taken so that the companies can remain competitive in industries which are ever-expanding, and more often include competitors from outside the United States. The workers who now are part-time or temporary workers often are among the newly self-employed who must find additional work to fill their work weeks and continue saving and investing for retirement on their own.

Planning Tips

Variable annuities are particularly good financial products to fund IRAs and SEPs because they can be purchased with flexible deposits to fit permissible contribution limits as they change year by year. They also free the self-employed person from active investment management so that he/she can devote the time necessary to build the business and produce current income. The variable annuity advantages of diversification, professional money management, availability of equity and bond accounts, ability to make allocation changes, availability of guaranteed accounts and annuity death benefits, and a variety of payout options, including annuitizing for life, are all together in one place.

SELF-EMPLOYED WITH EMPLOYEES

Self-employed persons who have employees, that is, small employers, have more complex considerations. Many are not in a position to make retirement plan contributions on behalf of their employees. This means that they cannot contribute for themselves except for IRAs (which have been expanded, as discussed in Chapter 11). The employer can assist employees in purchasing IRAs on their own by providing payroll deduction for that purpose.

There is a full range of qualified retirement plans. However, smaller employers, in a position to make contributions for employees or to offer matching of employee contributions, usually will want to stay away from plans that require the expense of extensive administration. Conventional SEPs and Savings Incentive Match Plan for Employees (SIMPLE) IRA plans can be used. There also are SIMPLE 401(k) plans which are easier to administer than conventional 401(k) plans.

Using variable annuities in these plans makes it possible for the plans to effect the advantages that larger employer plans, such as conventional 401(k) plans, have. There is the full range of investment choices, managed by professional managers, that many participants like; there is the ability to allocate investments and change allocations from time to time; guaranteed accounts usually are available; when payout time comes, there is the full range of withdrawal and income options at retirement; and there is the death benefit guarantee. It is hard to see how there could be a better package for the smaller plan.

SUPPLEMENTING EMPLOYER PLANS

It is argued that higher paid employees of employers with retirement plans are discriminated against because the combination of the retirement plan benefit and the social security retirement benefit is a smaller percentage of the employees' compensation before retiring than that of lower paid employees. The reason is that the higher paid employee's social security benefits are capped due to contribution maximums applicable each year. To have the same percentage of income at retirement, the higher paid employee needs to take other measures. The employer may have a supplemental retirement plan or deferred compensation arrangement. These are nonqualified plans with no plan contribution tax deductions available, although the employer may deduct benefit payments at the time they are made.

Definition

Not all employers are in a position to make contributions to nonqualified retirement plans and higher paid workers often need to save on their own. This is also frequently the case with respect to self-employed persons whether or not they have employees. Qualified retirement plans have contribution limits and if the self-employed person has employees, his or her participation is further limited. Sometimes, saving and investing on their own has appeal and logic to self-employed persons and smaller employers. Even though contributions to qualified retirement plans are income tax deductible, generally all of the income received is taxable.

On the other hand, personal savings and investment payments are not deductible but some of the money coming back will not be taxable. Generally, only the interest and earnings are subject to tax. And when variable annuities are used to provide periodic income payments, the nontaxable amount is spread over the income period, thereby subjecting only a portion of the income each year to tax, as explained further in Chapter 12. Not having to pay tax on part of your retirement income can allow the money to go farther. Again, the variable annuity advantages are there: convenience of purchase, diversification, professional fund managers, ability to change investment allocations, deferral of tax on interest and earnings, guaranteed accounts, death benefits, fixed and variable annuitization options.

TIMING THE TAX

We have been discussing a number of different segments and types of people interested in saving and investing primarily for retirement. Some people, although highly interested in solidifying their retirement income, are also quite interested in postponing all the income tax liability they can as long as they do not hamstring their ability to receive and use the income they need when they need it. Some of the tax havens of some years back, while certainly able to generate tax savings, turned out to be so inflexible that some people could not get to income when they needed it for unexpected expenses. That is not what most people want.

Successful people assume that their highest marginal income tax rate during their working years will be higher than their highest marginal rate after retirement. That is because they expect to have a relatively lower income after retirement, notwithstanding all their efforts to accumulate for retirement, and because indexing in the tax law gradually will move the rates upward to apply to higher numbers, plus the availability of extra exemptions at age 65 and other factors. So, waiting to take income, and the income tax that goes with it, until after retirement is a simple and straight-forward strategy. But an individual must not allow this approach to limit his/her options. He/she must be able to get to income before retirement if it is needed, even though tax will have to be paid on the income at this time.

Variable annuities have these abilities built in. While you are in the accumulation period prior to the time you begin to receive payouts on a regular basis, interest, earnings and gains in value of the investments held by the subaccounts are deferred for tax purposes. But if you need to withdraw money prior to payout time, you pay income tax on what you withdraw, to the extent of interest and earnings. If you are over age 59½, or if you qualify for one of the other exceptions to the 10 percent penalty,[19] there are no other income tax costs (although in the early years of an annuity a surrender charge may apply) and no need for any product redemptions or reconfigurations. The variable annuity goes on as before.

MAXIMIZING INCOME

Many people will enter their retirement years without having accumulated as much as they need or had planned to have. Although the reason often is that they did not or could not save or invest enough during their working years, there are other reasons. Financial emergencies, particularly those related to serious medical problems and disabilities, can both cause additional outlays of cash and limit people's income-earning capabilities. In some cases, unfortunate investment decisions will be made or there will be unwise major purchases. Sometimes, large, and not adequately insured, losses to property occur. The result is that the people have not accumulated enough to derive an adequate income from interest and earnings on the amounts accumulated. Yet, to start digging into principal amounts can be worrisome. That can be "a slippery slope." As principal is used up, the interest and earnings from the remainder are less. And with life expectancies increasing, who knows how long the income will be needed, how long the people will live? A long life should be a positive thing, but it cannot be if income dwindles to below a reasonable standard of enjoyment.

Planning Tips

While most people prefer to dwell on how much they can accumulate and how much income can be produced from it, the fact is, some will have a nagging concern over whether things will work out as well as they anticipate. It may be the case that these people will want to know, in some detail, how it is possible for the money they have accumulated to provide a maximum income that will last as long as they live. Annuities, especially variable annuities, offer solutions to this problem unlike any other type of financial services product.

The values in a variable annuity can be annuitized, essentially at any time. An annuity is calculated by combining the principal and any expected interest or earnings, for the time being considered, and spreading them out so that each periodic payment consists of some of each. These payments can be calculated to last for a certain period of time or for the life of the annuitant. The longer the payment period, the less each payment is; the reverse also is true. This life income feature is what makes annuities so valuable to people in their retirement years.

Once people reach a certain age and start a lifetime payout, the amount of income that an annuity will pay each month or each year for life far surpasses what could have been paid out each period in interest or earnings. People whose saving and investing have fallen short of what they would have liked are materially aided by the ability to have these larger income amounts. To be sure, since the periodic payments include principal as well as interest or earnings, the principal will be used up at the end of the period. That would not have been the case if only interest or earnings were paid out and principal were retained. However, if the income is paid for the life of the annuitant, there may be no overriding necessity for the principal to be retained. And the possibility of death soon after annuity payments begin can be ameliorated by use of guarantee periods and joint annuity payments. (See Chapter 7 for more details.)

To this point, the life income discussion has been cast in the framework of a fixed payout. Variable annuities also have variable payouts. Periodic payments are recalculated from time to time using the values in the variable subaccounts. Thus the periodic payments rise or fall with those values, making the annuitant able to continue a strategy of using variable accounts to track with inflation to the extent possible as time goes by. Either variable or fixed payouts may be used and the choice does not have to be made until it is time to start taking income.

RECEIVING LARGE SUMS

There are a number of people who will receive a large amount of money and will want and need to save and invest it for retirement and other needs. An obvious starting point is people who have inherited a significant sum of money. Then, some people will sell a house or other real or personal property of significant value; sometimes, it is the sale of the family home with a move into a retirement community or, perhaps, assisted living where housing is rented.

Additionally, a number of workers will receive severance package settlements, due to their agreement to retire early or due to their requirement to do so. While these people will need to use some of the money for living expenses, they may have a sizable amount which needs to be saved and invested for the future, once they have other employment or have decided to become self-employed.

Some people participating in employer retirement plans will determine that a lump sum is the best way to take their retirement proceeds. Most of the time, rolling the proceeds into an IRA, so that their tax position is preserved, should be considered. However, there may be some proceeds which should be taken on an after-tax basis and saved and invested. (More details are in Chapter 11.) People in business will sell their interests to others. Many of these arrangements will call for installments to be paid to the seller. Others will be subject to bank loans providing lump sums or relatively large amounts over a short period of time to the seller.

Sales Tips

Many of the people who receive these large amounts of money are not in a position to select individual investments. However, they are likely to be interested in diversification for safety, professional investment management while retaining the option to adjust the investment mix. In addition, these individuals may wish for some guarantees and appreciate the fact that the income tax on interest and earnings can be deferred to the time when proceeds are actually used and enjoyed. In short, variable annuities are excellent places for this money.

Of course, it usually is not possible to find whole groups of people who have recently received large sums of money to form a market for you, with the possible exception of participants in retirement plans or those being offered severance arrangements. But when talking with people about their future plans, it is a good idea to ask whether any of these events have taken place or will in the near future.

In addition to the employer retirement plans, especially plans of smaller employers, supplemental income plans, and the sale of business interests mentioned above, there are other considerations for variable annuities in business and estate planning. These subjects are taken up in Chapter 11.

CHAPTER FOOTNOTES

1.   Jim Connolly, "ICI Study A Portrait of 'Typical' Fund Investors," *National Underwriter*, Life and Health/Financial Services edition, August 19, 1996.

2.   IRC Section 72(q)(2).

3.   See IRC Section 72(e).

4.   Cheryl Russell, "Boomer Nest Eggs," *American Demographics*, July, 1995.

5.   Susan Mitchell, "How Boomers Save," *American Demographics*, September, 1994.

6.   B. Douglas Bernheim, "Who Will Pay for Retirement in the 21st Century?", *NAVA Outlook*, May/June, 1995.

7.   Cheryl Russell, "Boomer Nest Eggs," *American Demographics*, July, 1995.

8.   *Ibid.*

9.   Frederick Schmitt, "Study Finds Wide Gap Between Retirement Hopes and Savings," *National Underwriter*, Life and Health/Financial Services edition, May 6, 1996.

10. Charles Bierbauer, "When Boomers Go Bust," *AllPolitics*, March 10, 1997.

11. "A Reality Check from Retirees," *The Numbers News*, February, 1996, American Demographics, Inc.

12. B. Douglas Bernheim, "Who Will Pay for Retirement in the 21st Century?," *NAVA Outlook*, May/June, 1995.

13. *Ibid.*

14. Cheryl Russell, "Boomer Nest Eggs," *American Demographics*, July, 1995.

15. William Dunn, "The Eisenhower Generation," *American Demographics*, July, 1994.

16. *Ibid.*

17. *Ibid.*

18. Brad Edmondson, "The Next Baby Boom," *American Demographics*, September, 1995.

19. IRC Section 72(q)(2).

3

APPROACHING MARKETS

PRIMARY OR SUPPLEMENTARY MARKET?

When considering how you will go about marketing variable annuities one of your early decisions involves the level of intensity of the marketing you will be doing. Will variable annuities be one of a fairly large number of products you will be offering as a part of an overall plan? Or will annuities, including variable annuities, be lead products and major sources of earnings for you?

Supplementary Marketing

The practices of many variable annuity marketers result in a marketing approach where accumulation products (variable annuities, fixed annuities, mutual funds, perhaps other investments) play a significant role in their customers' future income plans but a relatively minor role in providing earnings to the sales representative on a year-to-year basis. That is, the sales representative may market life insurance and disability income to individuals and businesses as his or her primary business activity. He/she then markets accumulation products to those same individuals and businesses in order to provide a more complete service to them. When one of these sales representatives considers new persons to approach, an important consideration is that the persons be potential buyers of life insurance and disability income at some point in the not-too-distant future.

There is no mystery to the concentration on life insurance and disability income in these cases. The compensation which may be earned, as a percentage of the premiums paid especially in the first year, is far higher than is the case for accumulation products such as variable annuities. On the other hand, variable annuities are a good bit easier to sell, usually taking less time to accomplish, and sales are made many times more frequently. Consequently, many sales representatives prefer to concentrate on marketing variable annuities and other accumulation products.

Variable annuities are marketed by many persons who perform financial planning services for their customers. In many of these cases, the performance of the financial planning services is uppermost in the relationship with the customer. The services often are provided for a fee. The person performing the planning services may be compensated for the sale of financial products as well, or the planner's total compensation may be from sales of financial products. There are variations among the states with respect to permissible compensation arrangements involving financial planning services and purchases of financial products where both are provided.

Definition

In the two types of circumstances above — where the sales representative markets variable annuities as additional products accompanying life insurance and disability income purchases, and where the person provides financial planning services and markets variable annuities as part of the services provided — the variable annuities can be considered supplementary marketing. No additional or focused marketing is undertaken for the variable annuities; they are a part of the regular sales process taking place with the customer.

Primary Marketing

When, on the other hand, it is intended that variable annuities be a lead product and major source of earnings, things are quite different. It is necessary to reach a greater number of people, have many more transactions with people, and make many more sales. The reason is the relatively lower level of compensation for variable annuity sales. We will look at compensation levels in more detail in Chapter 9, but it is well known that the level of compensation per sale is such that it takes a great deal of premium to produce significant earnings.

As we have seen earlier, there are reasons this should be so. The public is much more interested in variable annuities than in life insurance and disability income. People are apt to see purchasing variable annuities more in terms of an opportunity than in terms of a duty. People know they need to accumulate for the future whereas they frequently have only a vague notion about insurance, no matter how often they may have had the subject discussed with them. As a result, there is a much higher likelihood of a discussion under favorable circumstances when the subject is variable annuities.

Following the more favorable hearing, variable annuities are much easier to put into effect. Although there is a need to determine that the variable annuity is suitable for the proposed purchaser, there is no underwriting in the insurance sense. Consequently, there are no physical histories or examinations, no attending physician reports, no blood drawn, or other tests. There is no wait for approval of the business. On the contrary, there is a need to get the business submitted immediately and for the contract to be delivered promptly after it is issued.

Targeting Markets

In order for you to make the greater number of sales needed, it is necessary that you have enough good people to see and have reason to see them. We have discussed reasons to see various classes of people, but here we are referring to having reasons to see particular people, or better, particular groups of people. When there is a group of people, which is accessible to you, with some characteristics in common, and needs that can be addressed by the products you have for sale, that is a market for you. It is even better if the people in the group communicate with each other because your favorable reputation can precede you and pave the way. A group of people you have targeted for attention is referred to as a target market.

Definition

Characteristics in Common

Money to Save or Invest. One of the characteristics that is desirable for people to have in common is some money that can be put in financial products for the future. For most, this is in the form of disposable income. For others, it is a sum of money from a non-recurring source, such as the sale of property or other asset, or from another financial product with which they are no longer satisfied, such as a low-interest-producing product or one that does not have potential for capital appreciation. So, to start you will want to look for people with money available. An obvious starting point is among those whom you have reason to believe are earning enough income to be in that position, or who otherwise show signs of relative affluence such as their home and/or neighborhood or the recreational and other activities in which they engage.

In the Same Age Group. Another characteristic in common is age. The people might be within a particular range of ages. When people are within a fairly small age range, their financial interests may be similar. Middle-aged people are more interested in planning for a retirement that is coming ever closer than are younger people. Older people usually are beyond the accumulation stage and are looking for ways of handling what they have accumulated. Younger people may be more interested in ways to maximize what little accumulation ability they have. Your approach to each of the various age groups can be different, emphasizing what is important to that particular group.

Planning Tips

Common Place of Employment. Those employed by the same employer have that characteristic in common. By learning about a company, you are in a position to know relative earnings of various groups, the fringe benefits available, and what opportunities the employees have for saving and investing through their employer. In time, you can learn who the more influential people are and, at least, something of what people's expectations for their future with the employer are. If you can become favorably considered by people employed by the same employer, you will have a powerful target market. This is all apart from whatever financial work you may be able to do with the employer. If you can work with the employer, either on a company basis or on a personal basis, your target market will be even more fruitful because of the prestige you will have built.

Type of Work. Another characteristic in common is the type of work the people do. People who do the same type of work tend to find each other and get together either formally or informally. Those doing the same work at a particular employer usually associate closely with each other. Those with different employers tend to get together through associations or less formal organizations. It often is the case that people doing the same type of work have other interests in common. Frequently, those of similar ages tend to associate more with each other than with others in the group. By learning about some of the people in a group, you can infer correctly about other people in many cases. You cannot rely entirely on these inferences but you can be in a much better position of understanding than you would have been with someone not a part of the group.

Principals of Businesses. Similarly, principals of businesses find each other in business organizations. The organizations may be for the purpose of sharing or exchanging information among the members or bringing in outside sources of information for education or consulting with members. It may be to promote the purposes of the member organizations by concerted public relations or marketing endeavors or by bringing political issues to the attention of members of local, state and national governments. In such business organizations, it is not unusual to find principals of businesses of similar sizes or of complementary enterprises working closely with each other. These characteristics in common attract the people to each other. When you learn about some of those who are principals of businesses, the knowledge will be useful with others similarly situated.

Common Interests and Hobbies. Social and service organizations can be targeted as well. People who have such things in common as hobbies, sports, high degrees of interest in music, literature, art, drama, good health, and religion tend to want to be together so they can discuss and enjoy their interests. The same is true of graduates of a college who belong to a local organization and of former members of college fraternities and sororities who belong to alumni and alumnae associations or chapters. Of course, these interests do not necessarily carry over so that the people have similar financial characteristics but those in the organizations tend to know more about most aspects of the lives of the people they associate with regularly than of other people. The common interests and knowledge of each other can provide a connection which can be the beginning of a target market for you. Then, if enough of the people have the financial characteristics and needs for your products, the organization can be a full-fledged target market for you. Service organizations can become target markets in much the same way.

Communicating with Each Other. In our definition of a target market, we mentioned the desirability of the people communicating with each other. This is because any favorable attitudes about financial products or the person(s) marketing the products will be communicated, thus lowering barriers for a marketing approach as well as increasing the likelihood that people in the group will take some of the initiative in seeking out information on the products. Where group members are situated near each other and have regular contact, the communication among them can help make the group be a very strong target market. Where the members do not communicate regularly, because they do not see or talk with each other on a regular basis, the group still is far better than marketing to the public at large because of the persuasiveness of the fact that members of the group with similar characteristics have become customers. Members of the group are aware they are in a position to seek opinions from members they do not know, though they do not make such contacts very often.

MARKET RESEARCH

A logical question is, how do you find out about the characteristics in common and the needs in common that the members of a group may have? The answer is, by doing research. Much of the research we have in mind would be done by surveying some persons you already know who are in a group you want to consider as a target group. If the persons you survey are your customers already, so much the better. They will know about the products and services you have available and you will not need to gain their confidence. And although some customers may have some reluctance about referring you to people with whom they work or with whom they socialize, their reservations usually can be overcome or their fears assuaged. Clearly, your customers among potential target groups are the best sources for your research.

People you know who are not customers are next best. They usually will be agreeable to listening to what you have to say. But it is important that you not leave out any of the steps you would use in approaching someone you do not know for information. That is, when you approach someone you do not know, you will want to have a well organized presentation that is brief, easily understood, and leads to a definite course of action. The course of action usually consists of the person supplying you with information about the potential target group.

As indicated, you can survey people you do not know, but that is harder because of the barriers which are placed in the way of seeing them under favor conditions. If you can get referred to them by someone you know, that is a big help. If you cannot, you still can survey them, of course, but your percentage of success in approaching and interviewing them will be lower than with those you know.

Survey Information

The survey should be designed to gather information on the group for your analysis so that it can be used to determine which groups will make the best target markets for you. The types of information you want will: (1) define the group; (2) list the common characteristics of the group members; (3) list the presumed financial needs of the members; (4) describe the extent and nature of the communication among the members; and (5) identify usable sources of member information, as discussed in more detail below.

1. *Define the group.* They can be described as employees of XYZ Company; owners of particular types of businesses or of businesses of a particular size; particular occupations or professions, such as accountants, account executives for advertising firms or pharmaceutical houses; members of golf or tennis clubs, or of social or religious groups. The location of the people is important; they should be in your target area. An important part of the definition is the number of people involved. There must be enough people in the group to be a viable market, especially considering the need for a large number of sales transactions.

2. *List the common characteristics of the group members.* Some of the possible characteristics were mentioned above: they have above average incomes; their ages are in the accumulation of assets years; the majority have children ten or more years from college; they are close to the point of taking distribution of their assets; they work for the same employer or at the same location.

3. *List the presumed financial needs of the members.* From what you have been told of the group and of common characteristics, what are the major financial needs to anticipate? Candidates are accumulation for retirement years, help with selection of financial products for saving and investment, efficient and effective distribution of assets they have or will have, business planning involving financial products, planned charitable giving, and tax planning.

4. *Describe the extent and nature of the communication among the members.* Frequent and significant communication is the best, but even occasional communication is better than little or none, assuming the people know each other by name and know some of the basic information about each other. When people know each other to some extent, they are more apt to

accept another person's recommendation or referral. When you hold a meeting involving more than one, there is comfort and validation among them that the meeting will be of value.

5. *Identify usable sources of member information.* You must have names, addresses, telephone numbers, and even fax numbers and e-mail addresses where appropriate. Membership and company directories are the best if they are available. Remember that such items must be used discreetly if distribution of them is not public. Telephone and street directories, CD ROMs, and the internet can be helpful when needed. Names, addresses and telephone numbers are starting points. Information on a company's employee benefits is available from the literature distributed to employees when members of your target group are employees of a particular employer. Information of a more personal nature usually is available only from the members themselves or from those who know them.

Analyzing the Data

The data you gather by means of surveys of as many members as possible of the potential target group can be supplemented with information which may have been published locally. Any materials published by the organization will help fill in missing information. The Chamber of Commerce will have some other information that has been published. The public library will have whatever newspaper and local magazine accounts there are. The idea is to get as much information as practicable on which to base your decision on whether to adopt the group as a target market.

Definition

Our definition of a target market began by saying the group is one that is accessible to the person doing the marketing. Obviously, you must be able to contact the members of the group, preferably with relative ease. Naturally, you can contact by mail anyone whose address you have. If you expect that they will take the initiative of coming to a meeting or otherwise contacting you, that may be sufficient, although many recommend following up meeting invitations with telephone calls to improve attendance. You can contact by telephone anyone whose telephone number you have. However, telephoning is becoming ever more problematic with the prevalence of answering machines and voice mail. If you can have an introduction or referral from a friend or associate, or from an employer, you stand a much better chance of getting through or getting your call returned. Accessibility to members of the group is an important aspect in your analysis. Without sufficient accessibility, you may not be able to put the other information you have to good use.

You can never have too much information about whether a group can become a target market for you but there is a limit to the amount of time and money you are able to spend collecting it. Once you have gathered the information with which to make a decision, it is time to analyze it. Can you gain sufficient access to enough people? Are there characteristics in common? Do the members appear to have needs which can be filled by the financial products you have to market? Do the members communicate sufficiently with each other? Can you get data on the members at a reasonable cost in time and money?

Having considered all of these things, are there enough people in the group to constitute a target market for you? Rarely will the viability of a target market be a completely obvious decision. There will be certain factors about which you are uncertain. You will have to make some assumptions subject to further developments and insights. Some of the assumptions will turn out to be accurate and some will not. Your analytical prowess will improve with experience.

Reminder

Although a few sales representatives or sales organizations are able to concentrate primarily on one group of people, because it is large enough and continues to add new members, most representatives and organizations believe they must have several target markets at a time. This is particularly true when you are marketing variable annuities and related financial products as lead products. You must have enough people to whom to market that the larger number of transactions and sales you need can take place.

As a Member of the Group

Getting involved yourself in one or more organizations has proved to be effective in developing target markets. Then, you can be your own source of data on the members and you can become known by them under favorable conditions. There is little problem with access to the members. Of course, these must be organizations of which you can be a contributing member. When these endeavors have been successful, several principles were observed.

Caution

Never become a member of an organization primarily to market your products. The members will recognize it quickly and will not like it. Become a member of an organization which has a purpose you truly believe in and want to support actively. Service organizations fit this definition but so do others, such as those devoted to literature, music, good health, certain hobbies, and the like. Purely social organizations may or may not.

What we are referring to are organizations that require you to work on worthwhile projects with other members. This will give you the opportunity to become well acquainted with people in a setting different from your usual setting. In many cases, these will be people you might have difficulty getting to see through a direct approach. After all, people of all sorts take part in projects for the good of others and to further their interests outside of their work.

Sales representatives often can take advantage of their people skills by working on committees to which some other members are not attracted. Most organizations always need more members and need to raise money. Working on those committees automatically brings you into consistent contact with many members of the organization and, because the work is important to the vitality of the group, it usually is appreciated.

When you work with other members, one of the things you want to accomplish is to learn about them and their businesses or professions and personal affairs and for them to learn about you. One of the especially good things about marketing variable annuities and related financial products is that the ups and downs of the stock market and economic news are always of interest and become topics of conversation. In fact, once people learn that you have some knowledge of such matters, you almost cannot avoid talking about them. The people will bring them up time and again. This means there will be ample opportunities to discuss topics associated with your work and to offer assistance. This is all to the good since contacting many people is the only way to have many sales transactions which can result in substantial variable annuity premiums sold.

OTHER MARKETS

Sales Tips

Some sales representatives build lists of potential customers without utilizing a target marketing process as such. One way is to collect names in certain categories. Many have found success in keeping track of the maturity dates of the certificates of deposit their customers and potential customers have. As long as CD rates remain relatively low, people are willing to listen to an explanation involving products with the potential for higher returns. They also are willing to listen to an explanation involving products that offer the opportunity for a reasonable level of participation in the stock and bond markets in order to retain purchasing power. Contacting the people on the list a few weeks before their CDs mature has resulted in moving the money to variable annuities in many cases.

In a similar vein, some sales representatives have found it profitable to keep track of the surrender charge period on the fixed annuities their customers and potential customers have. This is especially true of single premium fixed annuities, which often are considered by them to be similar to CDs in many ways. Once the surrender charge period has run, a transfer to a variable annuity may be made. And it usually can be made without recognizing any gain for income tax purposes. (All relevant tax aspects of the transfer should be considered. See the discussion of Code section 1035 transfers in Chapter 12.) Exchanges to variable annuities can offer the opportunity for participation in the stock and bond markets in order to retain purchasing power and the opportunity for higher returns.

Caution

But observe this caution. An individual who exchanges a fixed annuity for a new annuity, fixed or variable, incurs a new surrender charge period during which withdrawals are limited. The ramifications of this must be disclosed. Also, it is the position of the securities industry that an exchange of one variable annuity for another usually is not warranted.

SMALLER EMPLOYERS

A number of sales representatives have found success concentrating on smaller employers with whom they use variable annuities as a backbone of their retirement plans. As mentioned in Chapter 2, smaller employers know they need to have some sort of retirement plan for their regular employees, including themselves in many instances, in order to be competitive in attracting and retaining good workers. Labor markets go through cycles but any time unemployment is relatively low, competition for good people can be intense. On top of that, many smaller employers feel a responsibility toward their employees which includes at least some opportunity to participate in the tax advantages of qualified retirement plans to the extent possible.

A small employer may facilitate employees contributing to Individual Retirement Accounts or Annuities (IRA). If the employer is in a position to make contributions on behalf of employees or offer matching, there are conventional SEPs or Savings Incentive Match Plan for Employees (SIMPLE) IRA plans. There also are SIMPLE 401(k) plans which are easier for a small employer to administer. (More discussion of these plans is in Chapter 11.) Of course, the full range of pension and profit sharing plans is available, especially to larger employers.

Planning Tips

One of the things that makes variable annuities so appealing in these smaller employer plans is the fact that employees can have the range of investment choices that are so popular with conventional 401(k) plans. Yet, the employer is not burdened with the administration costs. Only a variable annuity can bring all of these choices and options in one convenient package.

This range of choices available to employees also makes variable annuities appealing with plans designed to supplement the employer's retirement plan. An employer may have a basic or modest retirement plan which many employees may need to supplement in order to build additional income for retirement. Employees can purchase variable annuities on a regular and consistent basis. The premiums for the supplemental variable annuities are not income tax deductible but the income when paid will be only partially taxable. For certain employees, the employer can increase compensation providing the means for making the additional purchases. Generally, it is better for the employer not to own and pay for the annuities directly as a supplementary income plan. (There is more discussion of these tax aspects in Chapter 11.) Where the types of choices available in the variable annuity resemble those available in the employer's basic plan, especially when it is a 401(k) plan, a certain degree of coordination and thinking in common are possible.

TAILORING THE SALES PROCESS

After you have decided on your marketing targets, it is time to tailor the sales process you will be using. Whether you use individual contacts, seminars, or other types of meetings as the initial contacts with members of your target market, the steps of the sales process are similar, even when they are executed in different ways:

1. The pre-approach by mail of one kind or another, by telephone, or in person.

2. The approach by telephone, in person, or at a meeting.

3. The gathering of customer financial information.

4. Analysis of the information gathered.

5. A presentation of needs identified and proposed solutions.

6. Implementation of solutions agreed to by the customer.

7. Any necessary follow-up and service after the sale.

8. Continuing service, follow-up and consideration of additional needs and solutions.

When you are approaching potential customers for variable annuities and related financial products one-at-a-time, the pre-approach and approach are similar to those used with other financial products. When you are using seminars or group meetings, they are different. The pre-approach is the invitation to attend the meeting, whether it is an open invitation or an individual invitation by mail or telephone. The approach is in two parts. First there is the invitation at the meeting (usually extended more than once) to complete a response card which requests a contact by one of the financial counselors or sales representatives present. Then, when the representative calls to schedule the appointment, the approach is completed. In these cases, assurance usually has been given to those attending the seminar that there is no obligation; for that reason, contacting people who have not come forward by responding may not be appropriate, although it is done some of the time. A different tactic is to invite those not responding to another seminar as a way of determining their level of interest.

The rest of the sales process, whether the potential customer has been contacted individually or has come to a meeting, is handled on a one-to-one basis. There may be some differences, however. A person who has asked to be contacted may have a definite idea of what he/she is interested in pursuing. Or he/she may be wary of a sales representative who attempts to go far afield of the representative's immediate interests and become involved in many additional financial considerations. When you sense that may be the case, it is best to continue along the path of the potential customer's interest and, after determining suitability, sell the product the person is interested in buying. Once you have gained your new customer's confidence, then you can go back and offer additional financial services and products. This is in keeping with the idea of having many sales transactions in order to produce a sufficient level of variable annuity premiums. (Of course, if it is your intention to perform more complete planning services before making any product recommendations, you will proceed differently.)

We also need to remember that the person who completes a form requesting a contact may have no idea of what he/she should be considering, notwithstanding the information provided at the seminar or meeting. Such a person probably will welcome an offer to do some financial analysis, including determining interests and risk tolerance, in order to get an idea of what sorts of products he/she should consider.

TIPS ON SEMINAR SELLING

Selling by using seminars to approach potential customers has become very popular and is in wide use. This is particularly true for selling financial products which have a certain degree of built-in demand such as variable annuities. Seminars involving retirement planning and/or accumulating for the future seem to have appeal for a large number of people. Seminars on estate planning or financial planning usually have not drawn as well although sometimes those attending are more affluent and, in some cases, better potential customers. Even though people probably should be interested in insurance planning, that is not a popular subject for seminars.

Committed to the Steps. Those successful at seminar selling make the point that a person can do well only by being committed, persistent, patient, and dedicated. The person must be committed to following the steps faithfully and not yielding to the temptation to take short cuts. He/she must have a system for keeping track of people who have been invited to seminars and who have attended. Since, for a variety of reasons, it may take several invitations to get the acceptance of some good potential customers, the system must provide for sending somewhat different invitations to the same people at proper intervals. The commitment must extend to planning and implementing a seminar or seminars that are worthwhile, suited to the knowledge level of the potential audience, and presented in a non-threatening atmosphere by qualified speakers.

Planning Tips

Be Persistent. The giver of seminars must be persistent. One of the major reasons for not achieving anticipated results through seminar selling is that the person stopped giving the seminars too soon. Many times this was a lack of patience and the expectation of results coming more quickly than they did. In retrospect, the seminars contained good enough information, the speakers were adequate, there were at least some good potential customers there (although often fewer than the seminar givers had hoped), and some sales contacts resulted. What was needed for success was more of everything. If the list of people mailed was a good one, things very likely would have been better after additional seminars.

Be Patient. Patience is not a word usually associated with many sales representatives of financial products. Yet, seminar selling requires it. If the representative short cuts the process, for example, by contacting people who attended and did not respond, it can poison the atmosphere if the group of people invited know each other. If those attending do not know each other, there may be less damage but, as was mentioned above, it often is better to invite people to other seminars. When someone has attended more than one seminar, it might be more appropriate at that time to contact this individual directly to offer additional services. Obviously, the person has more than a little interest in the subjects being discussed. Of course, you can only be sure a person has attended if you have a system for tracking attendance and any follow up mailing you might have done.

Invitation List

Reminder

Perhaps the most important key to the success of seminar selling is the list of persons you invite to attend. Who attends probably is more important than what is presented, although you will want to offer the best content and speakers you can. The more the people on the list fit in with those who are in your target markets, the better. After all, you would have designed the seminar for those types of people. When seminar givers are disappointed with the results of the seminars, it is most often the case that not enough of the right kind of people, or just not enough people, attended.

Lists of people to invite can come from a variety of sources. The closer you are to the people on the list, the more likely you are to be able to predict whether they will attend and how effective seminars will be. If you have a membership list of a target group, it will be a better list than one where you have only superficial knowledge of the people on it. Sometimes, sales representatives have success with lists of people they have contacted in the past but have never interviewed, assuming there had been good reasons to retain their names in the prospective customer files.

The business of developing lists from public sources using database management techniques has become more refined than ever. You can purchase lists with nearly any profiles. When selecting a company from whom to purchase such lists, there are several things to keep in mind. First, look for a track record. You not only will want to see the proof presented by the company, but will want to check out their references. If you know someone who has used the company, ask that person. Or you can begin with a referral to a company someone else has used with success.

**Planning
Tips**

Second, work diligently at giving a detailed definition to the type of people you want to appear on the list. Database management techniques today allow for multiple search categories. It is far better to get a smallish list of people who fit your target well than a large list, many of whom do not fit. This is especially true if you anticipate sending repeat invitations to people on the list, as many seminar givers recommend.

Third, expect to pay a fee commensurate with the value of the list. Sophisticated searches take more computer time and cost more. But the cost of the list is low compared to the time and energy you will devote to the seminars and you will want to have as much success as possible. A last point is that the information on these lists comes from public sources, for the most part. These sources sometimes are not refreshed as often as they might be and some of the information is somewhat out of date. To an extent, that cannot be prevented. Here again, the selection of the list-providing company is very important.

Caution

Some sales representatives have success with inviting people by newspaper advertisements and similar approaches. The people responding call a telephone number or mail a reply to the address shown in the ad. Although this approach has been successful for some, it usually is relatively expensive for the number of people who respond and finally attend. It also violates the principle of targeting your markets since the invitation is being extended to "the world at large." Many feel that is not the place to start with seminar selling.

Sponsored Seminars

Example

There are variations on seminar selling that have proved to be more successful, for the time, energy, and money invested, than the types of seminars we have been discussing. One of these is sponsored seminars. For example, a company with whom you or one of your associates has done business might be willing to sponsor a retirement planning or asset accumulation seminar for its employees, or for certain of its employees. In order to get company sponsorship, you will have to convince the employer that the information is worthwhile and needed by the employees and that it will be a positive experience for both employer and employee. What employers fear most is thinly disguised direct sales solicitations masquerading as seminars. It should be easy to assure the employer that there is no reason to fear aggressive tactics by explaining how the seminar is conducted and under what conditions employees are contacted following the seminar.

Sponsored seminars usually can be conducted at or near the employer's place of business. It is unusual for the employer to allow for time away from work for those attending, but seminars can operate successfully just following the close of work. Another approach is to have a series of shorter seminars at lunch time, with a box lunch provided. Here you are in a position to track attendance as an indication of interest in the topics being discussed.

Earlier, we discussed the fact that seminar selling often is abandoned before it has had a reasonable chance for success. Sponsored seminars need to be repeated from time to time and new ones, perhaps including some parts of old ones, presented. You must continue your presence in your target markets. Different people will be interested the next time; some of the same people will return, perhaps with more resolve this time to take action. If the seminar has been a positive experience for both the employer and the employees attending, it will not be difficult to schedule another after a reasonable period of time.

Some sales representatives have found the social, special interest, or service groups to which they belong receptive to seminars on some aspects of financial planning or explanations of various financial products. Many of these groups have regular educational programs and welcome the active participation of the members in one or more of them. Here again, there is the fact that these subjects are of interest to nearly everyone and are more likely than not to be well received. Obviously, the seminars or programs have to be conducted with the realization that those attending have not overtly expressed an interest in the subject. For that reason, your follow-up activities must be a bit more subtle. But there is no question you will have established your identity and shown some of your expertise among people in the group. Those factors are likely to prove to be invaluable.

Keep Promotion Going

Planning Tips

With respect to any groups where you have presented sponsored seminars or workshops or group programs, it is important that you keep promotion going afterward. If the employer or organization has a regular publication or newsletter, it usually will welcome well-written articles. When there is a tie-in to a recent seminar, it is even better, especially if some enthusiasm has been built among some of the people who attended. Those responsible for the publications may want to take advantage of the positive atmosphere concerning the seminar. If you feel able to write such articles, there is an abundance of ideas in the financial and trade press to inspire you. If you do not, distributors of variable annuities and other financial products produce a wealth of appropriate pieces which they will give permission to publish. What you are attempting to do is to keep the subjects discussed in the seminar in front of potential customers who then may take the initiative to approach you directly or indirectly. The articles also can pave the way when you approach them. Before we leave this subject, we should point out that sometimes it is possible to publish articles before the seminar takes place. This may improve attendance and establish some familiarity with you in advance of the seminar.

Designing the Seminar

Caution

When designing a seminar for the first time, there is a great temptation to "tell everything you know" about the subject in order to establish your expertise as the reason to want to contact you for assistance and guidance. That usually is the wrong thing to do.

There are two primary purposes for the seminar. The first is to give enough useful information to those attending so that they will consider the time well spent. This is not necessarily complex information. In fact, it is likely that it will not be. You want those attending to be able to go away remembering some of what was said. Relatively simple concepts and ideas are easier to comprehend and remember. One must keep in mind that, for the most part, it is people who have relatively unsophisticated knowledge of financial planning and financial products who respond to seminar invitations. Those who are well-versed or who have financial advisors usually do not consider that the time will be well spent. It is not a positive experience for most people to find themselves at sea trying to understand what is being said. Their minds will wander quickly.

The second purpose of the seminar is to make it easy for a person attending to sign a response card requesting a contact, or to ask individual questions of speakers or others or give opinions during breaks in the seminar program. In order to ask questions or give opinions, the people must feel comfortable that they understand what is being said. When someone hears something said with which he/she already is familiar, there is a validation of what is being said based on previous information. That is a very positive thing so long as there is not so much previously known information that the presentation appears to be trite. Considering these two purposes, the scope of the information provided in the seminar probably needs to be relatively limited.

The ideas that are presented can be of the same type you would use in sales interviews, e.g., information about why it is necessary to accumulate for the future, especially retirement, interest rate trends, the need for diversification and the like. Some of the ideas in Chapter 4 can be adapted for use. Other professionals, such as attorneys, can present information on estate planning, trusts, and advanced directives such as durable powers of attorney and living wills. The other professionals also are looking for opportunities to attract new clients and customers. Naturally, you will want what others say to be consistent with what you or your associates present. There must be good coordination so that things go smoothly. As we said, the problem usually is in limiting what is presented to what can be absorbed, rather than being concerned with filling the time available.

Absolute Must: Response Card

Sales Tips

There is one absolute must with respect to the content of the seminar. On several occasions during the various presentations, the speaker must call the attention of those attending to the cards which request information and/or an individual consultation. Logically, when a speaker has concluded discussion of a subject, he/she can invite, "If you would like to know more about this or would like to see how it applies to your own circumstances, note that on the response card (which is being held up) to receive an individual consultation."

It usually is better to make this suggestion at several strategic points in the program than to wait until the end. A seminar attender who is hesitant to complete a card, even though he/she knows there can be a benefit, can build momentum (or is it courage) to take action with the series of invitations. Of course, it is possible to overdo it resulting in resistance stiffening instead of softening.

Seminar information should be reinforced with a few, simple handouts, which also contain the name, address, and phone number of the person or organization presenting the seminar. Not only do the handouts illuminate the points being discussed, but they supply the names of contacts for more information.

Sometimes, a simple, fill-in outline of the entire seminar is used. This is not to say you should or should not hand out elaborate outlines or summaries of the entire seminar; some seminar givers do and other do not. The more elaborate handouts can distract the listeners from what the speakers are saying, robbing speakers of the opportunity to develop points in a systematic and sometimes dramatic and even entertaining fashion.

On the other hand, if you want listeners to acquire a substantial amount of information or to become acquainted with a procedure or process, such as a planning process, it might be preferable to use the more elaborate approach. With either approach, you will want to use an agenda indicating what subjects are being discussed during designated times.

Seminar Length and Speakers

Planning Tips

The length of the seminar is an important consideration. Again, there is the temptation to try to cram too much information into one seminar and the time needed grows longer and longer. Remembering the two purposes of the seminar, the time should be limited, and there should be breaks built into the total time allotment. Many seminar givers believe that two to three hours, including breaks, is about the limit. At the end, there should be time for those who want to linger to ask additional questions; this can be extremely valuable time for gently promoting contact with those presenting the seminar. Of course, if there are special circumstances, the time must be different. When you are presenting at lunch time or after work, the content and time must be adjusted to fit. And programs for organizations usually are expected to be shorter.

Reminder

It seems pretty basic to say but seminar speakers should be good presenters and able to answer questions without undue hesitation. You, as the seminar giver, should have a prominent presence but that does not mean necessarily that you need to be a major presenter. If you have the credentials and are at ease presenting, you can do so, of course. However, you can achieve a prominent position by introducing and credentializing the other speakers, handling question and answer portions, and the like. The audience must depart knowing who you and your business associates are and what you do, but there is nothing wrong with your having imported "outside experts" for the seminar. In subsequent interviews, you can refer to what certain speakers said even though you have said the same things in interviews all along. They will carry more weight having come from a seminar which your potential customer attended.

We have referred to the other business associates who may be present during the seminar. Some seminar givers conduct the program with only the help of any outside speakers and a person to handle the arrangements and logistics of the meeting. Others have business associates present, especially if more than ten or fifteen people will be attending. The other associates are introduced in their capacity to answer questions and listen to comments, and they have easily recognizable name badges. The people attending want to have easy access to someone to talk with when they are inclined to do so; they dislike waiting in line for too long. And any conversation is apt to improve chances that the person will ask to be seen individually. Besides, the associate who talked with this individual will have a reason to talk with him or her again later in the program or afterward.

ON BUILDING YOUR SALES PRESENTATION

Whatever the method of marketing, the sale takes place during one or more individual discussions with the potential customer. Earlier, we referred to the sales process which applies to the sale of variable annuities just as it does to most financial products. We also referred to the fact that there is a perception among many people of the need to accumulate for the future, especially retirement, and that products such as variable annuities have some level of built-in receptivity. The result is that people are more willing to discuss these matters than some others; you are able to get interviews with them more often. But they still will resist buying, and they will resist buying now in particular. It is not easy to agree to part with money, to make a financial commitment. If it were easy, the person being interviewed might have no money available by this time.

In building your sales presentation, you will want to take advantage of the built-in receptivity by coming to agreement with the potential customer about his or her interest in accumulating for the future. You may not have to prove that it is needed but you may have to give the customer some data on how much it might take. You may not have to prove that it is a good strategy to put some of the customer's dollars in products that invest in stocks and bonds as well as in guaranteed accounts, if desired, but you may have to provide some pertinent data on how to go about doing it and how you can be of assistance.

Perhaps the most important thing you need to learn is what is the potential customer's motivation for considering the purchase of financial products. Is he/she interested in "having the good life" or in not being poor? Are there specific financial goals? What is the relative importance of providing for the potential customer's spouse, or children, or grandchildren? How important is tax planning? Then, you will want to know about the customer's risk tolerance and need for access to the money being saved and invested. In short, what are the potential customer's needs which can be satisfied with variable annuities and related financial products.

NEED AND MOTIVATION TO ACT

You will want your approach presentation to hit the high points of the process you intend to follow to gather information and come to agreement on needs. When you have gathered the information you need to do an analysis; then, you will be in a position to identify needs and solutions to the needs. This can be a structured process extending over two or more interviews or it can be short, often concluding in the same interview because the needs are agreed to easily and the solutions readily apparent.

Reminder

When the process is to be a short one, the establishing of a need which your product can fill should not be short-circuited. Unless there is a need which must be filled, there is no motivation to act. Without the firm establishment of a need, the variable annuity purchase becomes akin to a commodity purchase. It is just something to consider along with a number of other things going on in the potential customer's life. If there is no motivation to act, then clearly there is no reason to act now, which so many times is the essence of the sale.

When the potential customer feels the motivation to fill a need, it is much more likely that he/she will want to act on it and remove at least one of the worries or concerns he/she has. There are other reasons to act now, such as the fact that investment markets are volatile or interest rates appear to be moving one way or the other. But the one that often proves to be the most powerful is the ability to resolve a problem or concern the potential customer has so that he/she can go on to other things.

The concept of packaging together funds, such as mutual funds, is an easy one for most people to understand but they sometimes do not have such an understanding of variable annuities. When presenting a variable annuity as the solution to one or more of the potential customer's needs, it is easy to get bogged down in detailed explanations of the product, leaving unsaid why the details are important to the potential customer.

Sales Tips

When all is said and done, the customer should understand, as fully as he/she would like to, the variable annuity he/she is purchasing. However, a sales representative must be careful that the discussion is not just of the product's features. The benefits that the customer derives from the features are what matter. You never want the potential customer to conclude that what he/she saw was a wonderful and flexible product for someone but not be able to see why he/she should be the one to buy it. It is a long established principle of selling that people buy benefits; they do not buy features.

4

SELLING IDEAS

FINDING THE DOMINANT APPEAL

Effective sales ideas are ideas that sell. An idea sells because it strikes a responsive chord with a customer; sometimes these are called customer "hot buttons." There may be a number of points which appeal to a customer, but there usually are just a couple which are dominant. Once you find one or more of these dominant ideas which appeal to a customer, you will want to concentrate on what you have found. You will need to cover other matters during the interview but it is important that you continue to emphasize the thoughts which appeal most to the customer.

Of course, finding the dominant idea usually is anything but "falling off a log." A customer will not volunteer that the point you have just made is important enough that he/she is apt to take action. It will be up to you to discern that from the customer's reactions and, perhaps, the intensity of the questions asked about the idea. Sometimes, you will misread a customer and concentrate on a minor issue for too long. Selling is an art, not a science; people frequently surprise you by saying or acting out things you do not expect. Dealing with people is not dull, to be sure. The good thing is that as long as you remain on positive terms with the prospective customer, you will be able to change directions and move to different sales points.

Research done among would-be financial services product customers has shown that people want information about products, services, and procedures. But they want the information provided in a convenient way. That is, they do not want to know "everything." In other words — they want to know what they want to know. And they do not want to feel they are being manipulated as they are receiving the information. We can take advantage of this understanding by being straight-forward, reasonably succinct, and by concentrating on what they find most helpful and appealing. And we should neither "talk down" to them, try to impress them with our "superior knowledge" of products and services, nor use manipulative interview techniques.

Caution

Would-be customers want to be in control and to engage in self direction with respect to the products and services they buy. Often, these can be exercised particularly when the people have a number of choices available to them. There are many opportunities for the variable annuity owner to exercise control and self direction; he/she has many choices which continue well beyond the initial choices at the time of purchase. A number of examples can be made known to the customer who wants to exercise such self direction and control.

Financial services product customers want to be able to trust the representative with whom they are dealing and the companies from which they are buying. Conducting yourself in a straight-forward, non-manipulative manner, concentrating on those things which are most important to the customer builds trust. Follow-up and follow-through add to it. Good and timely service from the issuing company builds trust with the company. Customer surveys have shown that most customers value highly a company which handles transactions accurately and in a timely fashion, and which is responsive to customer questions and requests.

Finally, customers are said to want fulfillment; that is, they want to feel they have accomplished what they have set out to accomplish. With variable annuities, there are ample opportunities for people to realize their ambitions for accumulating money for the future. There are numerous choices available which fit the risk tolerance of a particular customer. As stated, there also are ample occasions to exercise control and self direction with respect to the premiums they pay, the accounts they choose, the internal transfers they make, the withdrawals they use, and the payout provisions they employ.

In this chapter, we will put forward a number of sales ideas. We will do so by, first, stating the essence of the idea and, then, using some sample language in most instances. We will not attempt to fashion "complete sales tracks," for that would be a waste of space. Most registered representatives of even limited experience are happy to have a new idea, a notion of how the idea works, and something of how to say it. But they will take what has been provided and convert it into their own language and methods of showing and discussing it.

Reminder

More complete presentations are not shown here for another, perhaps even more important reason. Materials shown to a potential variable annuity customer must be approved in advance by the broker/dealer distributing the variable annuity. It is one thing to discuss general concepts; it is something else to show materials which are more particular to a specific variable annuity product. Compliance matters are discussed in more detail in Chapter 6.

Sales Tips

The eighteen sales ideas presented in this chapter include:

1.   Variable Annuities as IRAs: Building Retirement Income with Efficiency;

2.   Variable Annuities as IRAs: More Help for Children's Education;

3.   Importance of Regular Saving and Investing: Cost of Delay;

4.   Importance of Regular Saving and Investing: Dollar Cost Averaging;

5.   Maximizing Accumulation: Taking Advantage of Tax Deferral;

6.   Exercising and Maintaining Control: Having Many Choices;

7.   Exercising and Maintaining Control: Changing Investments;

8.   Exercising and Maintaining Control: Timing Income Taxes;

9.   Maintaining Purchasing Power: Investing in Equities;

10. Dealing with Risk: Using Diversification to Advantage;

11. Cementing Your Success: Strategic Use of the Guaranteed (or Money Market) Account;

12. Effective Income Planning: Defer, Withdraw, Annuitize

13. Keeping the Tax Penalty in Perspective: Don't Be Put Off By It

14. Handling Large, One-Time Amounts: Take the Pressure Off But Put the Money to Work;

15. Annuity Buildup Not Counted for Social Security Benefits Taxation;

16. Annuity Payout and Life Insurance Combination;

17. IRAs for Smaller Employers; and

18. Providing for Supplemental Retirement Income.

BUILDING RETIREMENT INCOME

Virtually all people are interested in hearing about, and perhaps acting on, ideas involving tax benefits to them. Few subjects are discussed more than taxes and any opportunity to pay lower taxes should be explored. The Taxpayer Relief Act of 1997[1] (TRA '97) changed some existing provisions and added important new ones in the areas of retirement and children's education — two areas of high interest to most prospective variable annuity customers. Let us look first at retirement.

Variable Annuities as IRAs: Building Retirement Income with Efficiency

Prior to 1998, many people had not been able to participate in Individual Retirement Annuities (IRA) on a tax deductible basis because they or their spouses were participants in other retirement plans and their joint incomes were too high. The deduction phase out began at $40,000 of joint income ($25,000 for an individual).[2]

TRA '97 made two far-reaching changes. First, the deduction phase out point was raised, to $50,000 in 1998 for taxpayers filing a joint return and will continue to rise in future years eventually to $80,000.[3] Second, when only one of the spouses is participating in a retirement plan, the spouse who is not participating may have a deductible IRA, beginning in 1998, so long as joint income is no more than $150,000.[4] This means that many more people are able to buy variable annuities as IRAs and deduct contributions.

And the usefulness of deductible IRAs has been further enhanced by the fact that the 10 percent penalty for premature distributions does not apply to distributions used for certain education expenses.[5] (More on that shortly and in Chapter 11.)

A new kind of IRA, referred to as a Roth IRA, was created by TRA '97, beginning in 1998. Contributions are not deductible but interest and earnings accumulate on a tax-deferred basis and when the proceeds are distributed, they are tax-free if the Roth IRA has been held for five years and the taxpayer is at least 59½ years of age.[6] Contributions made to Roth IRAs may be removed without tax for college expenses even when the taxpayer is under age 59½.[7] That is, it is considered that the first amounts distributed are contributions on which tax already has been paid. Only after all contributions have been removed will there be taxable distributions of interest and earnings. (More on these provisions in Chapter 11.)

Generally, people want all the deductions they can get in order to reduce their current taxes. They will be attracted to being able to take current deductions — the "a bird in the hand is worth two in the bush" philosophy. But tax-free income can be even better in the long run.

To illustrate, let us consider $2,000 per year at 7 percent interest for 20 years. The amount accumulated is $87,730; in 25 years, $135,352 is accumulated. With a deductible IRA, the person's cost is less because of the deduction ($2,000 less a 28 percent tax bracket deduction is $1,440), but the income is all taxable when it is distributed. With a nondeductible Roth IRA, the person's cost is the full $2,000 per year but the distribution is not taxed.

	Regular IRA	Roth IRA
20 Year Accumulation	$87,730	$87,730
28 % Tax on Distribution	- 24,564	- 0
Net Proceeds	$63,166	$87,730
Less Net Cost after Deduction	- 28,800	- 40,000
Total	$34,366	$47,730
25 Year Accumulation	$135,352	$135,352
28 % Tax on Distribution	- 37,899	- 0
Net Proceeds	$ 97,453	$135,352
Less Net Cost after Deduction	- 36,000	- 50,000
Total	$ 61,453	$ 85,352

Figures are derived from a compound interest table, the sum to which one dollar per annum, paid at the beginning of each year, will increase.

To be sure, these are simplistic comparisons. It is assumed that all distributions are taxed at 28 percent, which may not be the case. There is no calculation for the time value of paying the larger nondeductible amounts through the years. However, the plain fact is that tax-free distributions are worth a great deal. The overriding conclusion is that people should take advantage of these two types of IRAs to the extent they are permitted. Whether deductible or nondeductible, each spouse is limited to putting $2,000 into one type of IRA or another. Because of human nature, they usually will want to maximize what can be deducted first and then consider the other method of accumulating for the future.

Some sample language to use in presenting retirement planning ideas follows.

Sales Tips

M/M Customer, I am sure you are aware of IRAs, where a deductible contribution may be made to help you accumulate more for your retirement. You also probably are aware that because you participate in your employer's retirement plan, and because your family income is as high as it is, you cannot take an IRA deduction, even though the income limits have been increased. But do you know that because your spouse is not a participant in an employer plan, a deductible IRA can be set up for him/her? There is *a joint income limitation for that, too, but it is $150,000. Most of us are able to qualify with that kind of limit.*

Deductible contributions are great because when you send $2,000 to your IRA, you have to take only $1,440 out of your pocket if you are in a 28 percent tax bracket. The other $560 comes from a reduction in your income taxes. Or to put it another way, if you want to put $2,000 into savings or investments after taxes, you would need to earn $2,778 to have the $2,000 left after taxes.

Now, sometimes people tell me that this is all well and good but $2,000 a year isn't going to do much when it comes to retirement. These people are happy to learn about another kind of IRA now available (after 1997). They call it a Roth IRA and what is remarkable about it is the fact that though the contributions are not deductible, the income at retirement is tax-free — not a lower rate of tax, not part of it taxed. All of it is tax-free. That means when you take a $10,000 distribution, for example, you get to spend all $10,000 of it, not what is left after paying taxes, such as $7,200 in a 28 percent bracket. In your specific situation you can't have both a deductible IRA and a Roth IRA, but you have your choice for your spouse and the Roth IRA is available for you. Putting $4,000 each year into IRAs can be a big assist to your retirement income. Let me show you an example of how the two types of IRAs work. (Show an illustration similar to the one above.)

There is another valuable option for a self-employed person who does not have employees, perhaps a sales agent or representative or other independent contractor who essentially works alone. It is a Simplified Employee Pension (SEP), which allows for contributions of 15 percent (net of the contribution) up to a maximum amount.[8] Employees must be included in SEPs; hence, we are suggesting their use here for those without employees. Variable annuities may be used to fund SEPs. (See the discussion in Chapter 11.)

Employees of public schools and other non-profit organizations are eligible to participate in tax sheltered annuities (sometimes referred to as tax deferred annuities) on a salary reduction basis. They can put substantial amounts into these plans. Sales representatives who specialize in this area often service large plans in large school districts or large institutions, such as colleges or hospitals. (There is further discussion in Chapter 11.)

CHILDREN'S EDUCATION

Variable Annuities as IRAs: More Help for Children's Education

TRA '97 added or changed so many provisions affecting education expenses that parents and grandparents interested in assuring that sufficient money is available for their children and grandchildren at college time are faced with a dazzling array of programs and tax benefits. If anything, there may be too many choices to think about, a situation that often leads to inaction rather than action. Briefly stated, the list of choices includes:

1. The Hope Scholarship Credit, which can provide a tax credit of as much as $1,500 during each of the first two years of college, and the Lifetime Learning Credit, which can provide a tax credit for 20 percent of up to $5,000 ($10,000 after 2002) of qualified tuition and expenses during later college years, including post graduate education. The Hope Credit applies per student and the Lifetime Learning Credit applies per taxpayer. The credit amounts are indexed for inflation.[9]

2. An Education IRA, nondeductible contributions of $500 per beneficiary until the beneficiary's age 18. The proceeds will be received tax-free to the extent of "qualified higher education expenses," including room and board.[10] No contribution may be made to an Education IRA if any contribution is also made to a Qualified State Tuition Program (discussed below) during the year unless the contribution to the Qualified State Tuition Program is from the Education IRA. (Since the credits mentioned above are coordinated with other tax benefits available to a taxpayer, if the exclusion for distributions from an Education IRA is used, the credits cannot also be used in regard to the same expenses.)

Caution

3. Qualified State Tuition Programs which call for advance nondeductible contributions to a state fund and can be designed to cover most college expenses. These are state plans which generally call for purchasing credits which guarantee that future expenses will be covered.[11] Those participating in these programs cannot also contribute to Education IRAs.

4. Income tax deductions for interest on student loans, beginning at $1,000 and rising to $2,500.[12]

5. Distributions from deductible IRAs to pay for "qualified higher education expenses." The distributions will not be subject to the 10 percent penalty for premature distributions, although they will be taxable.[13]

6. Distributions from nondeductible Roth IRAs to pay for education expenses. Distributions to the extent of contributions made are returned tax-free since tax already has been paid. Interest and earnings distributed are subject to tax but not to

the 10 percent penalty when used to pay "qualified higher education expenses.[14]"

Qualified higher education expenses are tuition, academic fees, books, supplies, and equipment. For Education IRAs and Qualified State programs, they also can include room and board. Applicable limitations and exclusions are discussed in Chapter 11. The income limitations of deductible and nondeductible IRAs are discussed above. Phase out of the Hope and Lifetime Learning credits begins at a joint income of $80,000 ($40,000 for an individual).[15] The Education IRA phase out is at $150,000 of joint income ($95,000 for an individual).[16] Phase out of student loan interest deductions begins at a joint income of $60,000 ($40,000 for an individual).[17] Some of the phase out levels are indexed.

Reminder

As mentioned, there may be too many choices for many people. And it is important to remember that the situation in 10 or 15 years may be different from today. We all have seen tax provisions enacted, then modified in one way or another, and even eliminated or offset by another provision. Since credits are used during the college years, they must be available then. Having interest deductions for student loan interest is good but it is better if there are no loans for the graduating student or parents to contend with. State tuition programs may be useful and should be considered.

Sales Tips

What seems clear is that IRAs, funded with variable annuities, can be very effective in addressing education expenses. While provisions affecting IRAs may be changed in the future, the usual practice is not to take away tax benefits on amounts already contributed and accumulated. Add to that the fact that the same IRA being used for retirement can be used for education to a significant extent. This means that if, for one reason or another, some of the funds intended for education are not needed, they can remain in the IRA for retirement. And the decisions about using the money do not have to be made until college time arrives.

Following is sample language to use in talking about education funding.

M/M Customer, one of the financial concerns you have expressed is that your child (or grandchild) have the money to go to college, and even to graduate or professional school, if possible. I think you are right to have that in mind as something you would like to address. The latest figures I have seen, which happen to be for men, say that men between the ages of 25 and 34, who are just high school graduates, earn an average of $23,638. Those between 45 and 54 average $32,322. On the other hand, those in the younger group who are college graduates earn an average of $34,926. The older group averages $49,015. Doctorates and professional degrees pay off, too. The two groups holding doctor degrees earn $41,811 and $66,725 and those with professional degrees average $43,334 and $85,960, respec-

tively.[18] These are just averages, of course, but obviously, the investment in education is worth it.

There are a number of ways to accumulate money for college. One of them is tax deductible. Since your spouse is not participating in a qualified retirement plan as you are, he/she can set up an IRA for $2,000 per year and deduct it on your joint return. Money can be taken out for education. Then, you, or both of you if you decide not to use the deductible IRA, can set up nondeductible IRAs that provide for income at retirement that is totally tax-free. Obviously, tax-free income will go farther than income that will be reduced by tax. Let me show you an illustration of the difference. (Show the illustration of the two IRAs as above.)

With the deductible IRA, you can take money out at college time to pay for tuition, books, academic fees, supplies, and equipment. The money will be taxable but there is no penalty for taking the money out early as there used to be. With the nondeductible IRA, you can take out the money you have put in without paying any tax. If you take more than that, you will have some tax consequences so you may want to leave the rest in, to be taken tax-free at retirement.

With these IRAs, the same plans you are using for retirement can be used for many of the education costs you will have. You have flexibility because you don't have to dedicate certain contributions for retirement and certain others for education. You can do that, of course, but you don't have to.

REGULAR SAVING AND INVESTING

Most of the selling ideas used in the remainder of this chapter are designed to apply to variable annuities not being used in IRAs although the principles apply equally well when they are being used for IRA funding.

Importance of Regular Saving and Investing: Cost of Delay

Planning Tips

People have all kinds of reasons for putting off the saving and investing they should be doing. One of the most common is no reason at all; it is just not getting around to it. Sometimes, the lack of action is aided by too high or too low stock prices or by interest rates that are too low. An important point is that most people are better off when they do something, not when they do nothing. One way to dramatize the need to act is by showing the effect of the loss of interest compounding when saving or investing is delayed. Following is some sample language to use in presenting this sales ideas.

M/M Customer, you would not be unusual if you sometimes delayed saving and investing the money you wanted to. It's pretty easy to want to wait for stock prices to go down some, or for interest rates to rise, before making a commitment to save or invest. But financial experts tell us that delaying action can be very costly. The reason for that is the effect of the compounding of interest or earnings on investments over time. And delay costs us the time. Let me illustrate; I am not using any particular product, just illustrating a principle. (Refer to the chart in Figure 4.01.)

Figure 4.01

THE COST OF DELAYING IMPLEMENTATION OF AN INVESTMENT PROGRAM	
SCENARIO ONE: An individual begins investing $2,000 per year today and continues for 20 years.	
Amount Invested Annually	$2,000
Number of Years Invested	20
Total Investment	$40,000 **
Accumulation at 7% at Year 20	$87,730
Amount of Interest Earned ($87,730 - $40,000)	$47,730
Accumulation at 8% at Year 20	$98,846
Amount of Interest Earned ($98,846 - $40,000)	$54,846
SCENARIO TWO: Instead of beginning to invest today, the individual waits five years and then begins investing $2,000 per year and continues for 15 years.	
Amount Invested Annually	$2,000
Number of Years Invested	15
Total Investment	$30,000 **
Accumulation at 7% at Year 20	$53,776
Amount of Interest Earned ($53,776 - $30,000)	$23,776
Accumulation at 8% at Year 20	$58,648
Amount of Interest Earned ($58,648 - $30,000)	$28,648

Example

Example

** NOTE: Investing an extra $10,000 by beginning to invest $2,000 annually now instead of waiting five years produces an additional $33,954 assuming a 7% return ($87,730 - $53,776) and an additional $40,198 assuming an 8% return ($98,846 - $58,648).

Let us assume you want to put aside $2,000 each year for 20 years and can earn 7 percent on the money in some product or another. In 20 years, you *would have put aside $40,000 but your account would be worth $87,730. The extra $47,730 came from the compounding of earnings and interest.*

But now let us assume that you waited 5 years before starting to invest. At the end of 15 years, you would have invested $30,000 and your a account would be worth $53,776. The extra $10,000, invested at $2,000 per year for the first 5 years, produced an additional $33,954. Looking at it another way, if you decided you wanted to have the same $87,730 by the end of 15 years, you would have to put $3,263 per year in; that's 64 percent more. It's pretty clear that the sooner you invest and save with those products you choose, the better off you will be. As I said, this is not an illustration of any particular product and is not guaranteed. Your results will vary according to the performance of the accounts you choose.

For additional emphasis, a higher interest rate also may be illustrated in the belief that investments, which include a substantial equities component, probably will do better than 7 percent. The figure for $2,000 per year at 8 percent over 20 years is $98,846; in 15 years, the figure is $58,648. Thus, the extra $10,000 produces $40,198. The annual amount to reach $98,846 in 15 years is $3,371. Larger amounts are more dramatic, of course.

Importance of Regular Saving and Investing: Dollar Cost Averaging

Planning Tips

A major reason for delaying putting money into investments is waiting for the right time. The right time can arrive when higher stock or bond prices have dropped or when low prices have started to show signs of increasing. People attempt to "time the market" even though, many times, they deny that is what they are attempting. Yet, the fact is that if most people would begin investing, using dollar cost averaging, they would come out much better than if they waited for the right time, which often does not occur very soon.

Below is some sample language to use in discussing dollar cost averaging. (In this discussion, we will use the dollar cost averaging example shown in Figure 4.02. This same example is also discussed in Chapter 5.)

Figure 4.02

DOLLAR COST AVERAGING*			
Time	Premium	Unit Value	Units Purchased
1	$200	$10.00	20.00
2	$200	$12.00	16.67
3	$200	$ 9.00	22.22
4	$200	$ 7.00	28.57
5	$200	$10.00	20.00
Totals	$1000	$ 9.60 Average	107.46
* Charges against premiums, if any, have been disregarded in this example.			

M/M Customer, many of the people I talk with tell me they are tempted to put off making investments, waiting for an opportunity when the price has gone down a bit. What they often find is that they end up waiting for quite some time, and the money they intended to invest is left uninvested in the meantime. Many of these people have been happy to hear about the concept of dollar cost averaging and find that it makes a great deal of sense.

Example

The concept is this: you decide to make continuing investments of a specific amount at regular intervals. The result is that the equal dollar amounts buy relatively fewer investment units when the unit values are higher and relatively more units when the unit values are lower. In this example of investing $200 at each interval, we see that 20 units are purchased the first time when the unit value is $10. The second regular investment is made when the unit value has risen to $12 and so fewer units are purchased. By the time of the third investment, the unit value has fallen to $9 so that more units are bought. By the end of the five purchases in this example, 107.46 units have been purchased. With the unit value back at $10, the account is worth $1074.60, more than would have been the case if an equal number of units had been purchased each time.

One other point. The average unit value during the period was $9.60, but the average price paid was $9.31 ($1,000 payments divided by 107.46 units). This means the cost paid was $.29 per unit less than the average price, an added benefit of using dollar cost averaging.

As you might imagine, the success of dollar cost averaging is dependent in the long run on the performance of the investment being purchased. But it can take some of the stress out of deciding when is the right time to make investments. The truth is, the right time is regularly. Regular investing using dollar cost averaging has been successful for many investors.

Planning Tips

When a customer has a relatively large amount of money to invest, he/she still may want to use dollar cost averaging over an upcoming period of time and not invest all of the money in particular variable accounts now. Many variable annuities offer a provision for putting the large amount into a money market or other account and then making regular transfers to other designated accounts on a dollar cost averaging basis.

TAX DEFERRAL

Maximizing Accumulation: Taking Advantage of Tax Deferral

Earnings and interest in a variable annuity's accounts accumulate on a tax-deferred basis until they are withdrawn. This has the effect of paying a higher rate of return or increased earnings. The amounts accumulated are much more than would have been the case if the interest and earnings were subject to current income tax. When the interest and earnings are withdrawn, they are taxed and that must be taken into account when making the comparison between currently taxed and tax-deferred accumulations. And in order to present a complete comparison, the penalty for premature distributions should be mentioned. (We use earnings rates after taxes, a table of tax-exempt equivalents and a compound interest table to calculate the figures.)

Sales Tips

M/M Customer, many of my customers tell me that one of the things they like most about their variable annuities is the fact that the interest and earnings being credited to their accounts each year are tax-deferred; the customers don't have to pay a tax until they withdraw money, some time in the future. This means all of the yearly earnings are being credited and the people don't have to increase the taxes they are paying on account of it.

As you think about it, when you have to pay a yearly tax, as you must do with nearly all other savings and investments, it is as if the rate being credited has been reduced by the amount of the tax. If you get 8 percent on your money, but are in the 28 percent income tax bracket, it is as if you actually received 5.76 percent. Now, 28 percent is not the highest bracket, and you are or will be in a higher bracket, but let's look at that one as an example:

Example

$2,000 PER YEAR

	8 Percent	5.76 Percent
15 Years	$ 58,648	$ 48,378
20 Years	98,846	75,938
25 Years	157,916	112,446

By the end of 15 years we see a difference of just over $10,000. In 20 years, the difference is nearly $23,000 and growing. In 25 years, the difference has grown to over $45,000, quite a large amount. But, we have to remember that tax has been paid on the interest and earnings on the lower figure but not on the higher figure. Let's use the 20 year figure of $98,846. Of that, $58,846 hasn't been taxed yet. At 28 percent, the tax would be $16,477, leaving a balance of $82,369, still quite a lot more than the $75,938. The reason is that there have, in effect, been interest and earnings on tax savings during the 20 year period.

I should add a few notes to this. We have used a 28 percent tax bracket as an example; this may or may not be valid, we don't know. We do know that most people gradually move into higher brackets during their investing years and then go to a lower bracket during their retirement years. So, chances are, we are being rather conservative here. Another note is that we have assumed you would terminate the annuity at one time and pay the tax. That is not necessarily what you will do. In fact, most people plan to take income each year after retirement; the tax isn't paid all at once, and is deferred on the amount not yet received. Another option used by many people is to elect to receive income systematically over a period of years or for life; in that event, the tax can be spread over the period of payments. The final note is that we have assumed you would take your money after you are age 59½, a sensible assumption since we are discussing retirement. Any withdrawals you make before that age are subject to an additional tax of 10 percent to make up for the tax deferral you enjoyed while the money was being accumulated.

MAINTAINING CONTROL

Exercising and Maintaining Control: Having Many Choices

Sales Tips

As discussed above, people like to be in control of their financial activities and in a position to exercise self direction. Perhaps, one of the best ways to have control and self direction is for there to be many choices. Some people will make use of the many choices by being active in making changes and exercising options; others will be content not to do that, secure in the feeling that their affairs are being managed in their best interests. A way to dramatize the control that customers have is to speak of the benefits that the choices make available to them.

M/M Customer, many of my customers tell me that one of the things they like best about using a variable annuity in their investment programs is the fact that they can maintain control over how often they invest and in what investments. While financial experts point out how important it is for people to invest regularly, if they are to accomplish their objectives, it is comforting to know you are not locked in to investing a particular amount each month or each year. You may begin paying into the contract, and then stop for a period of time if there is a need for you to; then, you may begin again or you may begin paying a different amount. It's all up to you. As I said, you're not locked in.

When you start paying into the contract, you choose from among all of these accounts where your money should go. (Here you present the information on the guaranteed and variable accounts.) *As you see, there is a growth account, an aggressive growth account, a bond account, a balanced account with an allocation of stocks, bonds and other securities,* (and whatever other accounts are available). *This contract also has a guaranteed account which pays a stated rate of interest each year. Something else: all of these accounts are managed by professional managers; you can choose the managers who have the kind of experience you are looking for.*

These choices are yours to make. And the nice thing is you're not locked in here either. You are free to make changes in the allocation of the money you are paying. More than that, you can move money already invested into different accounts; and this happens without your having to pay taxes on sales, as would be the case with many other investments. Another option that is completely up to you is when to start taking income from the contract. I should point out here that there are some tax ramifications surrounding when you take income and you will want to take those into consideration.

There is another option that has been important to many of my customers. You have the option not to be so involved in making changes, as many people do who do not have the time or inclination to involve themselves more actively. You can "let things ride" pretty much as they are and feel content that the professional investment managers will do their best to maximize the returns on the accounts they are managing. After all, their performance records are important to everyone involved.

Exercising and Maintaining Control: Changing Investments

When the control matter is one less of having choices and more of fixing things when they do not go according to plan, the ease of making changes in the allocation of premiums and among the accounts is important to bring out. Sometimes, the automatic rebalancing feature (see Chapter 7) can be of comfort to those who do not want to be in a position to have to actively participate in making changes. The fact that all of the adjustments can be made without recognizing taxes on sales also is of importance.

M/M Customer, some of my customers like to watch their accounts closely and then make changes in them when they think it is time to go another route for a while. They are happy that they can make the changes without incurring any income taxes as long as they don't take any of the money out of the contract. Perhaps, you realize that with most types of investments, if you want to change from one fund to a different one, you can do that, of course. But you will have to do so by selling your interest in the one account and buying an interest in another. This means there will be taxes to pay on any gains during that year.

Planning Tips

What my customers like is the fact that they can move money from one account in the variable annuity to another without any tax consequence. In fact, the deferral of tax, as the values in the accounts continue to accumulate, goes merrily on. There may be some fees to pay but a certain number of these internal changes can be made each year without any fee. This moving of money makes it possible for these people to go that different route for a while with a minimum of fuss.

Naturally not all people like to be so active in making changes. Some like to pretty much "let things ride," content that the professional investment managers will do a good job. However, what some of these people find is that, over time, some accounts perform better than others because of economic conditions at the time. The result is that more of their investments than they intended are in particular accounts, whereas they had intended for the mix to remain pretty much as it was when they last made account allocations. These customers take advantage of our automatic rebalancing feature. What happens is that as often as you direct, money automatically is taken from one account and placed in others you have designated so that the allocations in the accounts you have selected are maintained. This rebalancing feature is yours to use as you wish; you can discontinue it at any time and resume it later. And note here, too, the rebalancing occurs without current income tax.

Exercising and Maintaining Control: Timing Income Taxes

Planning Tips

Most people are not given much control over when they pay taxes. Yet, a variable annuity affords such an opportunity through the tax deferral during the accumulation period and taxes payable only on withdrawals and payouts when they are taken. This is no small point in the "scheme of things" for many people. To point it out in the context of control over what is happening is a good tactic.

M/M Customer, I am sure you have noticed that, each year in the late fall, articles appear in all the newspapers and magazines describing tax planning tactics. So many of the tactics can be used only by a few people, especially those with businesses of their own. The rest of the readers can only wish they had more opportunities. A variable annuity gives you at least one more opportunity. The money you put into the variable annuity accounts accumulates earnings and interest each year. But you do not have to pay income tax on the accumulated earnings each year so long as they are not taken out of the contract.

Someday, and certainly at retirement since a variable annuity is a long-term product particularly suited to supplementing retirement income, you will want to start taking money out. The years you will want to take the most out are the years when your other income is the least. This means that you will be paying income tax at a lower rate than if you took the money out when your other income was higher. In fact, you may choose to take little or none out in the years when your other income is particularly high. And what you don't take out continues to accumulate on a tax-deferred basis. I haven't seen that tactic mentioned in those articles on tax planning very often, but I think you will agree it is a good one and one you can use yourself. I need to point out that I have focused on retirement since there usually are some tax consequences if you withdraw money before age 59½.

Retirement also affords you another tax tactic. When you reach retirement age, one of your options is to take an income for life; with that option, less of the income you receive each year is subject to tax; more of it is yours to keep. When and if you decide to use this option is completely up to you. When the time comes, you will want to look at the figures for the various ways of taking income and make the decision that suits you best.

MAINTAINING PURCHASING POWER

Maintaining Purchasing Power: Investing in Equities

Everyone agrees that a savings and investment program must take account of inflation. Sometimes, it is less known that in order to have returns greater than inflation, some of the investing must be in equities and/or bonds; this means some element of risk. Younger people are not especially averse to risk; they become more concerned as they get older when there will be less time to recover from an unfortunate investment. People can purchase variable accounts with investments in stocks and bonds with varying risk profiles; they also can purchase less risky accounts.

M/M Customer, inflation has been mild over the past few years but I am sure you remember or know about the late 1970's and early 1980's when it was a lot higher. And you know that inflation is a major concern of financial markets and of regulatory bodies such as the Federal Reserve Board. Whether inflation is rising or falling, its effect over the years has been substantial. It is estimated that it takes nearly five times as much money today to have the same purchasing power as thirty years ago. As you contemplate your saving and investment plans, no doubt you want to factor in some consideration of which kinds of investments have done well compared to inflation.

Generally speaking, over the past 50 years small company stocks have far outstripped inflation; large company stocks, those usually referred to as "blue chip" stocks, have done almost as well. Even long-term government bonds are somewhat ahead. Treasury bills have run about parallel to inflation. What this tells us is that in order to run ahead of inflation, you must invest some of your money in stocks, such as the ones in several of the accounts in our variable annuity.

Planning Tips

As you know, past performance is no assurance of how accounts will perform in the future. There is some element of risk connected with investing in accounts owning stocks; they can go down as well as up. But the past record appears to confirm that the best hope of keeping up with and even doing better than inflation is with a portion of your money in stocks. The nice thing is that you can allocate as much or as little as you like to one or more of the accounts holding stock; you can change your mind as often as you like and you can move more money into those accounts or move some out, all without having to sell shares and pay taxes.

DIVERSIFICATION

Dealing with Risk: Using Diversification to Advantage

A number of investors, especially first-time investors and older people, are concerned with keeping risk at a low level. For many people, low risk levels translate principally into guaranteed interest rates. While making use of the guaranteed account is a good tactic, it can be overdone, especially when people forget to consider the other way of dealing with risk—diversification. Diversification within and among the variable accounts allows the variable annuity buyer to address risk while still investing in accounts that can appreciate in value, thereby possibly hedging inflation.

M/M Customer, some of the things you have said give me the sense that you are concerned about the risk of investing in variable accounts, which are the ones that have the potential for appreciating and keeping up with inflation. That is not unusual; I hear it frequently. Often, the people are just more comfortable with guaranteed interest rate accounts even though they continue to worry about future inflation. What we have here is the risk of losing your principal pitted against the risk of losing some of the purchasing power of the money you are saving and investing.

Planning Tips

Many financial experts point out that the risk of losing principal can best be addressed by diversifying your investments. When you diversify, you invest in many different types of investments — stocks of various types, corporate bonds and government securities, and so on — and many different investments within each of the types. When one investment goes down, another goes up; when one industry has a slow down, another is doing pretty well; when one major product or service becomes less popular, another sells particularly well. Diversification, these experts say, is the way to deal with many of the risks of investing.

It is hard for an individual investor to diversify; he/she doesn't have the money to make enough investments fast enough. But an individual investor can diversify with the variable accounts in a variable annuity. Each of the variable accounts has investments in any number of different companies and organizations; one of the criteria that the investment managers use in selecting what to buy is maintaining diversification. Then, you can do your own diversifying; you can allocate your money among as many of the variable accounts as you like. And if you take a look, later on, at the accounts you own and decide you want to change to achieve more diversification, you can do that easily and quickly.

USING GUARANTEES

Cementing Your Successes: Strategic Use of the Guaranteed (or Money Market) Account

Sometimes, we must remind customers that it is all well and good for the values in variable accounts or other investments they own to increase; they have nice gains on paper. But gains are not realized until the investments are sold and the money received. Until that happens, the paper gains can go away as the values or prices fall. As customers contemplate the gains, they must consider whether to stay invested as they are, awaiting further gains, or get at least a portion of the money out and realize the gains. When there are taxes to pay on the sales, the dilemma can get worse. Strategic use of the guaranteed account or the money market account offers ways, unique to the variable annuity, of dealing with the situation. (Note that there may be limitations on amounts which may be transferred in or out of the guaranteed account during any one year.)

M/M Customer, when the account value of one of your variable annuity accounts or the price of another investment you own has increased substantially, you have a nice gain, a happy thought indeed. But some of my customers have said this otherwise happy situation can pose a bit of a dilemma for them. They know that they must sell the investments and take the money if they are to realize the gain. Otherwise, the investments' value may fall. On the other hand, the investments may continue to rise and they will wish they hadn't sold. Adding to this is the fact that, with most investments, the gains from the sales they will make are subject to current tax. If the investments go down, they don't feel so bad about the tax because they have made a smart move. But if the investments continue to rise, they feel doubly bad because they are not in the investments any more and they have had to pay taxes.

Example

A variable annuity gives you the opportunity to cement your successes by moving money out of some accounts and into others without a current tax to pay. For example, you could move a portion of the money in a variable account that has risen in value into the guaranteed account (or money market account). Then, if the value of that variable account should fall, you have the money out, earning a guaranteed rate of interest (in the guaranteed account). If the value continues to rise, too bad, but at least you haven't had to add insult to injury by paying a tax on the gain. And another nice thing: when you perceive that the value of the variable account is on its way up again, you can move some of the money back into it. (I do need to call your attention to one more point: there is a limit on transfers involving the guaranteed account, etc.).

INCOME PLANNING

Effective Income Planning: Defer, Withdraw, Annuitize

When a person considers various sources of income from savings and investments, both during the working years and at retirement, it frequently is the case that planning the amounts to receive at various times and under various conditions is difficult. Apart from knowing the unknown, there is the fact that so many financial services products do not offer a range of choices which includes not taking income and deferring the tax, taking as much as you need, and maximizing income later through annuitizing. Of course, all of those choices are available with a variable annuity.

M/M Customer, in our discussions, you have indicated that the income you will be able to receive, later on, from your savings and investments is of high importance. Most of my customers feel the same way. They also tell me that they very much like the idea of being able to control the income flow so that they can make the best use of it. What they mean by that is this: During your working years, what is most efficient is not to have to report as taxable, income you don't need and intend to leave accumulating in order to build up your future accounts. Around retirement time, what is most efficient is to be able to take just what income you need and pay taxes on it. What you don't need, you leave accumulating for the future and don't pay taxes on it. Then, later in your retirement years, in the event you have not been able to build up as much as you would have liked, what is most efficient is to have the option to get the absolute maximum income from that which you have accumulated.

That is what you have with a variable annuity. During your working years, values accumulate but you are not expected to pay taxes on any of it unless you take some of it out. At retirement, you may withdraw as much or as little as you like, and the rest will remain accumulating without any tax being recognized on the gains. Then, if for some reason you would need more income than you would be able to realize from interest and earnings alone, you can elect an income option. Typically, the amount of income is equivalent to the amount you might receive from interest earnings as high as 10 or 12 percent or more. The income comes from a combination of principal and interest and lasts as long as you live. Under that arrangement, the principal is used up, but the income, which can be either fixed or variable at your option, is paid to you for as long as you live and will serve you well. Arrangements can be made so that payments are continued to someone else if something happened to you within just a few years. (A comparison of one or two annuitization examples, with what can be withdrawn yearly while maintaining principal, can dramatize the value of annuitization, something not available with most other financial services products.)

PENALTY TAX PERSPECTIVE

Keeping the Penalty Tax in Perspective: Don't Be Put Off By It

Some people considering the purchase of variable annuities are put off, perhaps even frightened, by something that sounds pretty ominous—the penalty tax on premature distributions. Not surprisingly, the issue often is raised by those competing against the purchase of the variable annuity; for dramatic effect, they make the penalty tax sound nearly like the impugning of the character of the annuity owner. It is spoken of as something akin to the sword of Damocles hanging ready to seriously wound the unwary. Yet, the fact is, it is only a tax, one of 10 percent. It seems foolish to put off the benefits of tax deferral and the many other benefits of owning a variable annuity just for that.

M/M Customer, several times now you have mentioned the 10 percent penalty tax which comes about when withdrawals are made from variable annuity accounts before the owner is age 59½. I think we should discuss it for a few moments. First, Congress put the extra tax in as a kind of balancing weight to compensate for the tremendous value of being able to defer income taxes on the interest and earnings in the variable annuity accounts during all the years leading up to the time when a person starts taking regular income at or near retirement. The deferral results in much more money being built up than if the interest and earnings were subject to tax each year as they are with most savings and investments. (Here, an example similar to "Maximizing Accumulation: Taking Advantage of Tax Deferral" discussed above might be used.)

But let us suppose that you do have a need to withdraw money from your variable annuity before age 59½. The tax is assessed against the amount of money which is included in income. If you withdraw in the early years, not all of the money you withdraw may be interest or earnings; the amount that isn't is principal and not subject to regular or penalty tax. If you withdraw later, all of the amount withdrawn is likely to be interest and earnings and subject to tax. But the tax is being assessed only on the amount you take out, not some larger amount, not the entire amount of interest and earnings. The amount not withdrawn remains with its tax deferral in place, still a much better position than if you had had to pay taxes each year as they accrued.

And why would you decide to make a withdrawal prior to a time near retirement? Isn't it either because you need the money due to a temporary loss of income or emergency, or because you have an unusual opportunity? If you have a good opportunity, the extra 10 percent will be worth it. The point is, the 10 percent tax is there but it should be kept in perspective. A great many annuity buyers will never have occasion to deal with it. Those who do are apt to find it more an annoyance than anything else. And all agree that it is not all that big a price to pay for tax deferral on accumulations.

LARGE, ONE-TIME AMOUNTS

Handling Large, One-Time Amounts: Take the Pressure Off But Put the Money to Work

Sales Tips

Surveys of nonqualified annuity buyers have shown that quite a large number of people buy with proceeds from one-time events: an inheritance, the sale of a home, farm or business, an insurance benefit, a bonus, or a gift from a relative. They do so because they want to use the money to bolster retirement income. But they also do so because annuities offer a place to put the money to work without the people having to make a lot of difficult financial decisions within a short period of time. Quite often, this type of event will not come along again. Perhaps more than anything else, the people are fearful of making mistakes which will cost them money that never will be replaced. That motivation may be more powerful than any desire to "make a killing" by means of "brilliant" investments.

M/M Customer, surveys have shown that many buyers of variable annuities are people who have (inherited money from their parents, sold their businesses, etc., whatever is the case) as you have. Most often, the reason is that they can relieve themselves of having to make a whole series of financial decisions all at one time; yet they can put the money to work right away, rather than leaving it in a checking or saving account while they fret over what to do with it. Nobody likes to be rushed into making these types of decisions; the more rushed you are, the more likely you are to make mistakes. After all, it's not as if these opportunities come along every day.

With a variable annuity, you can put some of the money into those accounts you know enough about to have some confidence. Then, you put the rest into the VA's money market account or the account which pays a stated rate of interest. When you have satisfied yourself that you want to move some of the money out of those accounts and into others that might produce higher earnings, you just do it, no muss, no fuss. You can take days to decide; you can take weeks; you can take months or years. It's up to you. And the thing that makes this even better is the fact that once you put the money into the variable annuity, whatever accounts you choose, the income earned from interest and earnings is not subject to current tax. The tax is deferred until you take the money out of the contract. This means that you don't even have to pay extra income taxes while you do your investigating and research about where to put your money. (If the guaranteed account has limitations on internal transfers, that fact should be brought to the customer's attention.)

When people retire early, whether by their own choice or otherwise, they sometimes receive a cash settlement or, perhaps, their retirement plans are such that the proceeds need to be rolled over, probably into an IRA. These people have the same concerns as those just discussed, except that the rollover to the IRA must be done according to certain rules. See Chapter 11 for more on distributions from retirement plans and related subjects.

SOCIAL SECURITY BENEFITS TAXATION

Annuity Buildup Not Counted for Social Security Benefits Taxation

The buildup of funds inside an annuity is not counted for determining what is called "provisional income" with respect to the taxation of social security benefits at retirement. For most taxpayers, provisional income is the sum of adjusted gross income, tax-exempt interest, excludable U.S. savings bond income used for higher education, and one-half of social security benefits received at retirement. If provisional income exceeds a threshold, which is $44,000 for couples filing jointly or $34,000 for single taxpayers, an income tax must be paid on up to 85 percent of the social security income. When the full 85 percent of social security income is taxed depends on how much the benefits are and how much provisional income they have.[19]

Example

For example, if a couple receives $20,000 of social security income during the year, 85 percent of it is taxed if they have provisional income of at least $56,941. There is a formula for determining how much is taxed. The fact that the buildup inside an annuity is not counted means that an annuity might be a better choice for someone to use for saving and investing than, say, tax-exempt securities, where interest is included in provisional income. The closer the couple's income is to $44,000 and below $56,941 the better.[20]

ANNUITY PAYOUTS AND LIFE INSURANCE

Annuity Payout and Life Insurance Combination

As discussed in Chapter 7, an owner-annuitant may elect to take an income for life. The amount of income depends on the person's age and sex and whether a guarantee is provided for another person. Couples frequently elect to take joint and survivor income payments so that the payments will last as long as either of them lives.

Planning Tips

When joint and survivor income is elected, the amount of income is usually considerably less than if income were to last for the life of the annuitant alone. In some instances, it can be shown that the person might be better off to take the higher income and use a portion of it to buy a life insurance policy for the benefit of the person who otherwise would be the joint annuitant. This can be the result where, for example, the beneficiary is considerably younger. It is also true that if the second person predeceased the annuitant, the higher income would continue for the life of the annuitant and the life insurance could be used for another purpose. How much and what type of life insurance and when it is feasible to consider this approach depend on the amounts needed and ages of the people involved.

As discussed in Chapter 12, when someone elects a life income payout, only a portion of it is subject to income tax each year; the rest is a return of the investment in the contract.[21] Some annuity owners decide that they will take withdrawals at retirement, rather than a life income payout. They want to do this so that the principal they have accumulated in the annuity can be left to their families. These withdrawals will be subject to current income tax until they exceed the amount of premiums that have been paid into the annuity contract.[22] Therefore, these individuals might be better off to elect a life income option, with only part of the income subject to tax, and buy a life insurance policy for the benefit of their families. The premium for the life insurance would come from the savings resulting from lower taxes. For those who have an estate planning need, there would be no annuity value includable in the person's estate at death and the life insurance policy could be owned by someone other than the annuity owner or by an irrevocable life insurance trust, presumably keeping the proceeds out of the estate.

SMALL EMPLOYER RETIREMENT PLANNING

IRAs for Smaller Employers

Smaller employers, who want to provide their employees with a retirement plan that is affordable and easy to administer yet has some of the attributes of larger plans, have a new tool — SIMPLE (Savings Incentive Match Plan for Employees) IRAs. These plans are salary reduction plans, which means the employer already is paying the portion of the contribution being made by the employee. The employer then makes a matching contribution on a dollar-for-dollar basis up to 3 percent of compensation, but the match is provided only for those who contribute. There is an alternative arrangement for making smaller contributions for all employees.[23] These plans may bridge the gap between employers who feel unable to have any plan and those who are able to do so. (Further SIMPLE IRA information is in Chapter 11.)

Employers who feel unable to provide even a SIMPLE IRA plan sometimes take steps to facilitate employees purchasing their own individual IRAs. Through their payroll systems, the employers arrange to withhold personal IRA contributions so that they can be put into the employees' individual plans. By doing so, they enable employees to save for the future by taking the money out of their paychecks before the employees receive them. The employers must be sure that they remain in a position of doing this as a convenience only and that they not acquire any fiduciary responsibility with respect to the money being withheld as might be the case with a qualified retirement plan.

Providing for Supplemental Retirement Income

Most businesses find it desirable to provide some sort of supplemental retirement income for their more highly compensated employ-

Planning Tips

ees, quite often as an incentive for those employees to remain with the business and not look elsewhere. For a smaller business, a popular way of doing so is by means of a bonus arrangement with the employee, who often also is one of the owners of the business. Under such an arrangement, the business increases the compensation of the employee (by bonus or otherwise) so that the employee can purchase a variable annuity or other financial services product. The extra compensation is tax deductible, provided that it is reasonable compensation,[24] and the employee includes it as additional income. The employee's cost is the tax on the added income. In some instances, additional compensation is given with which to pay the tax.

Another way of providing supplemental retirement income is through the use of deferred compensation arrangements or supplemental retirement plans. With these arrangements, there is no current deduction available to the business but the business builds in some restrictions on when the employee receives the compensation. When the contract between the business and the employee operates to remove the restrictions and the employee receives income, the business may take a deduction and the employee includes the income. The business usually owns the funding financial services product. Because of the "nonnatural person" rule which applies to annuities, variable annuities usually are not used with these arrangements. Life insurance often is used when the arrangement is started far enough in advance for the cash values to accumulate adequately.

Caution

The bonus plan and supplemental retirement plans, as well as the "nonnatural person" rule, are discussed in Chapter 11. Also discussed in Chapter 11 are several estate planning aspects of annuities, including annuities which are not of the usual commercial variety.

AFTER THE SALE

One final point relating to providing service to a customer, perhaps, long after the sale—those representatives who have many annuity customers frequently receive calls from their customers relating a financial emergency, need or opportunity which the customers must address. These customers, under age 59½, are disappointed when they are reminded of the 10 percent penalty tax applicable to withdrawals. They begin considering other ways of getting the money they need.

It is important to remember the thoughts raised above under "Keeping the Penalty Tax in Perspective." Depending on the particular circumstances, the penalty tax may turn out to be a reasonable price to have paid for the benefit of all the tax deferral on accumulations over the years. The admonition is, "Do the math." Get the facts before jumping to a conclusion that the values in the variable annuity are beyond reach until age 59½. In the long run, it seldom is a mistake to save and invest money regularly, especially in a product as versatile and dynamic as a variable annuity.

CHAPTER FOOTNOTES

1. The Taxpayer Relief Act of 1997, P.L. 105-34, enacted August 5, 1997.

2. IRC Section 219(g) prior to amendment by TRA '97.

3. IRC Section 219(g)(3)(B) as amended by TRA '97.

4. IRC Section 219(g)(7) as amended by TRA '97.

5. IRC Section 72(t) as amended by TRA '97.

6. IRC Section 408A as added by TRA '97.

7. IRC Section 72(t) as amended by TRA '97.

8. See IRC Section 402(h)(2).

9. See generally IRC Section 25A.

10. See generally IRC Section 530.

11. See generally IRC Section 529.

12. See generally IRC Section 221.

13. See generally IRC Section 72(t).

14. See generally IRC Sections 408A, 72(t).

15. See IRC Section 25A(d).

16. See IRC Section 530(c).

17. See IRC Section 221(b).

18. "The Big Payoff in (College) Degrees," *Forecast*, November 1996, American Demographics.

19. See generally IRC Section 86.

20. See the following article for a helpful treatment of this subject. Ivers, James F. III, "Planning for Older Taxpayers with Nonqualified Deferred Annuities," *Journal of the American Society of CLU & ChFC*, November, 1995.

21. IRC Section 72(b).

22. IRC Section 72(e).

23. See generally IRC Section 408(p).

24. IRC Section 162(a)(1).

5

MARKETING AND SALES SUPPORT

ACHIEVING CUSTOMER SATISFACTION

When marketing and selling variable annuities, a major goal, perhaps *the* major goal is to come as close as possible to achieving customer satisfaction. Customers are most likely to be satisfied when two things occur. The first is when they, in fact, do save and invest money as planned, rather than remaining on the sidelines gathering information and hesitating to take action. People worry about making mistakes and, as a result, put off acting. Often, they do not understand that when they do not act by saving and investing, they are acting not to do so.

The second occurrence leading to customer satisfaction is when they save and invest in a satisfying way. By a satisfying way, we mean that customers understand the reasons they are selecting to purchase what they are purchasing and they understand how they will benefit from the performance of what they select. A satisfying way may also include the convenience of the purchasing method as well as the services provided by the sales representative and his/her office and broker/dealer. Later on, customer satisfaction is retained and enhanced by good service after the sale including timely and informative reports and other communications.

Not every product in which a customer invests will turn out to be a winner. Some will perform at levels that are less than expected or less than average. At these points, if customers know and understand the reasons they selected the particular accounts, they are in a better position to "stay the course" with what they have, at least for the time being, or to make the shifts in allocation of accounts which are more likely to give them the satisfactory results. What does violence to customer satisfaction is not being pleased with the results at hand, not understanding why those accounts were the ones they selected, and not knowing what to do about the situation. In fact, the people may feel worse off than they did before they made their purchases, even though they really may be better off from an objective standpoint.

EXPECTATIONS FOR THE FUTURE

There are many sides to customer satisfaction, including expectations for the future. With the benefit of hindsight, we can see several reasons why the expectations of investors might be out of line. From 1926 to today, the compound return, with dividends reinvested, for the S & P 500 is at an annual rate of 10.7 percent. Yet, in the past twenty years, the rate has been 14.6 percent. As a result people have begun to think of 14 or 15 percent as normal.[1]

Similar developments have affected thinking on the volatility of equity markets. Measured by the standard deviation, more recent market volatility is about a third less than it has been over the past 70 years.[2]

All of this means that the work you do with a customer to get him/her to commit to putting a certain amount or continuing amounts into a variable annuity and the work you do in helping him/her select accounts among which to allocate the premium is of great importance. You start out knowing that your customer may have at least somewhat unrealistic expectations about the performance of the accounts, based on mostly recent information. The customer also may have little patience for the inevitable ups and downs in account values. For these reasons, you need to call on support information, concepts and tools designed to inform him/her and provide a basis of understanding for the financial events which will follow.

MARKET TIMING

Definition

Many articles are written about the difficulty of attempting to "time the market" — that is buying when prices are at their low points and selling when they are at their high points. Those potential investors who are not frozen in place, and actually do act, often miss the lows and highs, sometimes by a substantial margin.

And, if money is being held in liquid, but low-interest, accounts awaiting action, there can be a further loss. Occasional savers and investors often do poorly in the market because they react to a kind of herd mentality. Large numbers of purchases take place, following extensive publicity about the success of stocks or accounts, resulting in the purchases being made at or near the high for the current period. And many occasional investors sell near the low points due to a generalized fear of falling prices and further exercise of the herd mentality.

DOLLAR COST AVERAGING

The opposite of trying to time the market is making regular and consistent premium payments. This approach allows the customer the

Definition

opportunity to engage in dollar cost averaging, a most important concept. Dollar cost averaging is paying a fixed amount of premium at regular intervals — monthly, quarterly, semi-annually, annually — regardless of the unit values of the selected variable accounts (or the current interest rate on new premiums paid into the guaranteed account). The equal dollar amounts will result in relatively fewer variable account units being purchased when unit values are higher and more units when unit values are lower. Figure 5.01 illustrates the mechanics of dollar cost averaging.

Figure 5.01

DOLLAR COST AVERAGING*			
Time	Premium	Unit Value	Units Purchased
1	$200	$10.00	20.00
2	$200	$12.00	16.67
3	$200	$ 9.00	22.22
4	$200	$ 7.00	28.57
5	$200	$10.00	20.00
Totals	$1000	$ 9.60 Average	107.46
*Charges against premiums, if any, have been disregarded in this example.			

In Figure 5.01, $200 of premium is paid into a variable account each period of time. The unit value of $10 at the time of the first premium payment results in 20 units being purchased. As the unit value goes up, fewer units are purchased. When it goes down, more units are bought. For ease of calculation, we bring the unit value back to $10 at the end so that we can look at what has happened. Since 107.46 units have been purchased and each unit is worth $10 currently, the value in the account is $1,074.60 at that point.

There is an automatic benefit to dollar cost averaging due to the fact that more units are purchased when unit values are lower and fewer when unit values are higher. As we see from Figure 5.01, the average unit value at the time of purchase was $9.60. But the average cost of a unit purchased was $9.31 ($1,000 premium divided by 107.46 units), a $.29 per unit gain. This gain is always the case with dollar cost averaging and the more volatile the accounts, the more gain there will be. Of course, the unit value of the account must eventually at least regain the starting level for the gain in units to be of beneficial effect.

Planning Tips

It can be argued that dollar cost averaging greatly reduces the stress involved in investing in accounts that can fall in value as well as rise. It is particularly useful when purchasing variable annuities because the customer can pay premiums in convenient, regular amounts and designate accounts in which the premiums are to go. The variable annuity owner can change the allocation amounts going to particular accounts or change his/her selection of accounts. Sometimes, the principle of dollar cost averaging can help give a prospective customer the confidence to begin making regular payments into the contract.

Dollar cost averaging can also be used to reallocate money already in the variable annuity contract. As explained in Chapter 7, some variable annuities provide that the owner may direct the regular movement of funds from one account, such as the money market account, into other variable accounts on a regular basis, e.g., monthly, quarterly. The reallocation continues until there is no longer money in the account from which reallocation is being made or until the contract owner directs that dollar cost averaging be discontinued.

ASSET ALLOCATION

Definition

In the early chapters of this book, we discussed the need for a potential customer to diversify investments and savings primarily to achieve safety. With diversification, the downs of one investment might be offset by the ups of another. Some of the risk and uncertainty of investing could be reduced, a defensive strategy. But there is another side to diversification and it has to do with achieving the customer's objectives. In this context, selecting different kinds of investments is referred to as asset allocation. It involves identifying the mix of assets that will produce the desired results while maintaining a balance between risk and return.

With asset allocation, the customer is not seeking to maximize return in the usual sense but to obtain the maximum return that can be had while keeping risk at an acceptable level. If we could predict which investments or class of investments would perform the best over a period of time, asset allocation would not be needed. But since we cannot predict with certainty, we select asset categories and determine what percentage of the total will be in those categories. We will not eliminate fluctuations but we can reduce the fluctuations of assets in the aggregate while moving toward our objectives.

Asset allocation can be used both in a long-range way and in a manner that is more short-range. Viewed at long range, the customer can establish an asset allocation which will remain unchanged until some major changes occur. Along the way, he/she may need to rebalance accounts so that the allocation remains as has been decided. In the short range, from time to time, the customer may want or need to make modest changes in allocation to achieve better returns. There come times when long-range changes must be made. For example, when the person who has been accumulating for retirement reaches that age, he/she may need to change to an allocation with more emphasis on income and less on growth.

ASSET ALLOCATION MODEL

A useful tool to help a potential customer decide on an asset allocation is an asset allocation model. There are a number available, some of them in computer programs that present allocations with charts and graphs. Most ask for answers to a series of questions from which a possible asset allocation is derived. The asset allocation models represent that what they are presenting is one possible strategy based on the responses to the questions. They should be viewed as broad guidelines and any investment decisions should come after a careful examination of the person's own situation and circumstances and careful review of the prospectuses and other materials associated with the financial products being considered.

The questions asked in asset allocation models are those having to do with:

- The person's investment objective

- How long a period of time is available to reach the objective

- The person's age grouping

- The person's income tax bracket

- The importance of current investment income

- How much cash reserve the person has

- How important inflation is to the person

- Future prospects with respect to current income and assets

- The person's tolerance for risk and volatility

- The person's tolerance for asset loss

The answers are scored and the possible asset allocation percentages are presented. In one allocation model program, three of the possible allocations are shown in Figure 5.02.

There are other possible allocations from the particular model program used in Figure 5.02. As the explanation of the program indicates, the allocation is just one that is possible. The portfolio choices usually refer to broad classes and not to the particular accounts in any one variable annuity or to any particular mutual fund.

The potential customer's own likes and dislikes will overrule anything suggested by a computer model. For example, the poten-

Figure 5.02

ALLOCATIONS FROM MODEL ASSET ALLOCATION PROGRAM			
	Growth	Conservative Growth	Income
Capital Preservation (Guaranteed Acct., Money Mkt.)	5%	23%	30%
Income (Corp. & Govt. Bonds)	10%	16%	28%
High Yield Bonds	8%	5%	10%
Growth & Income Portfolio	24%	20%	12%
Growth Portfolio	23%	11%	5%
Aggressive Growth Portfolio	15%	11%	5%
International Portfolio	15%	14%	10%
Total	100%	100%	100%

tial customer may not care for high yield bonds or international stocks and, when all is said and done, he/she may particularly like several of the portfolios in the variable accounts for one reason or another. Nonetheless, a suggested allocation can do much to focus the person's thinking and help him/her decide which actual accounts to choose.

Planning Tips

We have been referring to the asset allocation model as part of the process whereby the customer purchases the variable annuity. A model can be used earlier in the sales process as well. When approaching a potential customer, you can offer it as a service in helping him/her decide whether a variable annuity might be appropriate for consideration. Use of an asset allocation model also can be offered to those attending seminars. Or, a shortened version can be used as a part of the seminar.

PERFORMANCE HISTORIES

When deciding on the purchase of a variable annuity, a buyer is or should be interested in the provisions of the contract itself and in the various accounts he/she might select for the allocation of premiums. Performance histories and records of past performance can be quite useful in the selection of accounts. The broker/dealer distributing the variable annuity will provide past histories and performance data as well as information about the accounts' money managers and the company issuing the annuity contract. Detailed information on the contract is in the prospectus. We will take up prospectuses later in this chapter.

THIRD PARTY SOURCES

In addition to the account information available from the broker/dealer, there are a number of third party sources which may be used to learn about the variable accounts. Because there are so many more mutual funds to report on than variable annuity accounts, most of the information available has to do with mutual funds. But there is considerable variable annuity account data which can be obtained. Following is a sampling of what is available. It is not a complete listing.

Morningstar, Inc. This company has data available in both print and electronic media. Morningstar concentrates its attention on selected funds. In some reports, there are 1,500 funds considered and in others there are over 6,000. With fewer funds, the reports are more detailed, include more analyses, and take up more factors than would be possible if more funds were included. Funds are given ratings.

Lipper Analytical Services. This service tracks the performance of about 32,000 funds worldwide and its data are often quoted in the general press, financial press and on television. There are numerous performance rankings but not as much analysis as the sources which report on fewer funds.

Value Line. Published by Standard & Poor's, Value Line extends the S & P stock analysis and reporting methods to mutual funds. The reports are detailed, much as Morningstar, and ratings given are based on a combination of performance criteria.

CDA/Wiesenberger. The publication is the oldest one reporting performance, investment management, and historical data. The reports are published annually.

Since these publications are concerned primarily with mutual funds and the variable accounts in variable annuities, less information is provided on the annuity contract itself. Rather complete summaries of contract provisions, as well as listings of investment options, are available from *The Variable Annuity Research and Data Service* (VARDS). VARDS information includes fees and charges, premium minimums and maximum issue ages, transfer and withdrawal data, and other contract features. It also includes the ratings of the issuing companies from the independent rating services.

INSURANCE COMPANY RATING SERVICES

Reminder

Since variable annuities are issued by insurance companies, on their own or in partnership with mutual fund or other financial services companies, the financial ratings of the companies, by independent rating agencies, is of importance. The ratings are not quite so important as they are when life insurance and fixed annuities are being considered, chiefly because the variable accounts are separate from the general assets of the insurance company and free from the claims of its creditors. However, the ratings are important with respect to the guaranteed or fixed accounts which are supported by the company's general assets. And should a company have financial problems, some of the services and procedures being provided might have to be curtailed. We will discuss four of the rating services here.

A. M. Best Company. The oldest is the A. M. Best Company which has published *Best's Insurance Reports* since 1906. The objective of Best's rating system is to evaluate the factors affecting overall performance of an insurance company in order to provide an opinion as to the company's relative financial strength and ability to meet its contractual obligations. A large number of companies are rated by Best although some are not assigned ratings due to unique or unusual business features.

Moody's Investors Service. A credit research firm founded in the early part of the century, Moody's began rating debt securities of insurance companies in the mid-1970's. It introduced insurance financial strength ratings in 1986 to provide institutional and retail investors with objective and independent credit opinions. Life insurance company ratings are called financial strength ratings and are opinions of the company's ability to repay punctually its senior policyholder claims and obligations. Moody's rates just over 150 U.S. companies and fewer than ten Canadian companies but these are the largest companies in terms of reserves.

Standard & Poor's. As mentioned above, Standard & Poor's has been providing ratings of financial strength and credit quality for more than 70 years; it assigns ratings to debt issues of a wide variety of municipalities and corporations throughout the world, including insurance companies. In the early 1980's, S & P extended its rating business to include the claims-paying ability of insurance organizations. About 250 companies are rated via a comprehensive process and nearly 1,000 more are assigned a claims-paying rating using a quantitative process.

Duff & Phelps Credit Rating Company. Operating internationally, Duff & Phelps has been providing investment research to institutional clients since 1932. It began offering insurance claims-paying ability ratings in 1986. Ratings also are provided for bonds, notes, debentures, preferred stocks, commercial paper, certificates of deposit, structured financings, and sovereign financings.

The rating designations used by the services differ but the patterns are similar. Where one has high-end ratings of AAA, AA, and A, other services use Aaa, Aa, and A, or A++, A+, and A. The pattern is for all the services to have ratings which they describe as superior, excellent, and very good, or exceptional, excellent, and good, or highest, very high, and high.

These high-end ratings differ somewhat from each other but all are considered to denote financially secure companies. There may be lower ratings than those just mentioned which also are secure. But below those are ratings which the services describe as vulnerable or uncertain or possessing risk or questionable, etc.

Except for the ratings which are assigned from quantitative data, e.g., S & P's assigned claim-paying ratings, the methodology of determining ratings is similar. The companies submit considerable data on many operational and marketing aspects of their operations as well as supplementing the financial data which may be obtained from public sources. As a rule, the services confer with management and financial representatives of the companies for further development of the information. The ratings themselves are arrived at independently and published. The companies pay to have the ratings determined.

THE PROSPECTUS

One important document in the variable annuity sales process is the prospectus, which is looked on alternately as very helpful and something that must be endured. Though efforts are underway to bring simplification, most prospectuses are highly detailed and quite lengthy. But the fact of the matter is that the prospectus must be presented at or in anticipation of the first contact with the potential customer when a variable annuity product is to be discussed.

Definition

The prospectus contains a complete description of the workings of the contract and the various accounts, albeit in language some consider to be more legalistic than necessary. When comparing one contract with another, the prospectuses are valuable sources of information. There should not be any significant information about the contract and accounts left out. Rather than treating the prospectus as a necessary evil, some registered representatives use highlighted portions of it to explain the contract and the accounts. They feel that by doing so, they portray themselves as capable of handling complex information and able to make it relatively easy to understand. They can reinforce the veracity of the briefer, more eye-catching sales materials they are using.

Most prospectuses begin with broad descriptions of the contract and the accounts in which premiums will be invested. These descriptions can include definitions of terms to be used and a summary of:

1.   Contract provisions — workings of the contract, premiums, units of purchase, transfers, etc.

2. A summary of the various accounts offered.

3. Contract fees and charges.

4. Account fees and expenses.

5. Summaries of performance data of the accounts.

Following the broad descriptions are elaborations and more detailed explanations. With respect to the variable annuity contract, there are explanations of :

1. Premiums, units of purchase, crediting, valuing of units.

2. Transfers among accounts, limitations, rebalancing.

3. Surrenders and withdrawals.

4. Charges — contract fees, mortality and expense charges, surrender charges, waiver of charges, etc.

5. Death benefits.

6. Fixed and variable payout options.

If the contract is used in qualified retirement plans, there is some discussion of pertinent information. Disclosures, e.g., an IRA disclosure, sometimes also are included.

Each of the fixed and variable accounts is described; those sections include:

1. Investment objectives and policies of the account.

2. Account expenses.

3. Financial summaries including investment activities, asset values and expense ratios.

4. Risk factors applicable to the account.

5. Other investment information such as participation in futures contracts, options, repurchase agreements, etc.

6. Information on the investment advisor and fees charged.

In addition to the proprietary funds of the annuity contract issuer, many variable annuities have variable accounts managed by outside investment advisors. These accounts also must be described in the same detail and usually are housed in the same prospectus or attached to it. However, although the same types of information are included as those describing the proprietary funds, the formats often are somewhat different.

TRIAL PROFILE

The complexity of prospectuses has been a subject of considerable discussion over the years. No one is very happy about the situation, and that includes the Securities and Exchange Commission whose chairman has called for improved and more understandable disclosure to investors.

Definition

At this writing, the SEC is permitting the use of a "profile" to accompany variable annuity and mutual fund prospectuses for a trial period. The SEC hopes the profile will contribute to efforts to find ways to enhance investor understanding of variable annuities and investor ability to compare competing variable annuity products. The commission is optimistic that it will contribute to knowledge of how to improve disclosure, through the profile itself or, more generally, through changes to the full prospectus.[3] As things stand, the profile is to accompany a prospectus and not supplant it. Everyone's hope is that someday a profile or other simply-written document can be used for disclosure and the prospectus, as it is now known, can be replaced.

There are several versions of the profile, covering some or all of the following items:

1. The fund's goal.

2. Investment options.

3. Investment strategies.

4. Risks.

5. A description of an appropriate investor.

6. Fees and expenses.

7. Investor services and inquiries.

8. Purchase information.

9. Fund performance (including in chart form), comparative indexes.

10. Redemption information.

11.   Disbursement information.

12.   Fund advisor data.

13.   Taxes.

The list of topics is rather extensive and it is clear some time will be required to come to consensus on what language to use and how much to say about each topic. It is also clear that the SEC will not allow the discontinuance of the use of prospectuses until something capable of replacing them comes along. Meanwhile, marketers are looking to the day when it will be possible to prepare, print and distribute fewer and less voluminous documents to prospective customers. Since that day does not appear to be right around the corner, it remains necessary for marketers to be familiar and at ease with prospectuses in their current form.

SALES ILLUSTRATIONS

Sales illustrations are used with most insurance and annuity presentations. When explaining a fixed annuity or the fixed account of a variable annuity, projections into the future may be shown, using the current rate and the guaranteed rate. Projections of assumed interest rates also may be used so long as the current and guaranteed rates are illustrated as well. A sample illustration of this nature appears in Figure 5.03.

With these illustrations, you may design retirement income scenarios and show how the various withdrawal and fixed payout options might work. A National Association of Insurance Commissioners (NAIC) model regulation on sales illustrations of fixed annuities is in the process of being developed for adoption by the various states.

Caution

The variable accounts are another matter. No future projections involving the variable accounts may be shown. A portrayal of illustrative amounts of premium put into the variable accounts in the past, and remaining or continuing for ten years to today may be shown. With these portrayals, you are in a position to illustrate amounts of premium being discussed with the potential customer in order to give your discussions more realism. But, of course, you never may imply that the situation will continue to be the same; in fact, you must make a point of saying it is very unlikely to be the same.

We should point out here that the rules applicable to variable annuities and those applicable to variable life insurance and variable universal life insurance are different. With the life insurance products, you may use hypothetical interest rates projecting into the future to illustrate the variable accounts. The rates you may use are limited to

Figure 5.03

| | | | SAMPLE VARIABLE ANNUITY ILLUSTRATION FIXED ACCOUNT ONLY | | | |

FOR: John Taylor
AGE: 45

YEAR	PREM.	TOTAL NET PREM.	GUAR. CASH SURR VALUE	GUAR. ANN. FUND	PROJ. CASH SURR VALUE	PROJ. ANN. FUND
1	10,000	10,000	9,925	10,800	9,925	10,800
2	2,400	12,400	12,617	13,596	13,230	14,256
3	2,400	14,800	15,438	16,476	16,855	17,988
4	2,400	17,200	18,392	19,442	20,831	22,020
5	2,400	19,600	21,485	22,497	25,186	26,373
6	2,400	22,000	24,721	25,644	29,956	31,075
7	2,400	24,400	28,886	28,886	36,153	36,153
8	2,400	26,800	32,224	32,224	41,637	41,637
9	2,400	29,200	35,663	35,663	47,560	47,560
10	2,400	31,600	39,205	39,205	53,957	53,957
11	2,400	34,000	42,853	42,853	60,866	60,866
12	2,400	36,400	46,611	46,611	68,327	68,327
13	2,400	38,800	50,481	50,481	76,385	76,385
14	2,400	41,200	54,467	54,467	85,088	85,088
15	2,400	43,600	58,573	58,573	94,487	94,487
16	2,400	46,000	62,803	62,803	104,638	104,638
17	2,400	48,400	67,159	67,159	115,601	115,601
18	2,400	50,800	71,645	71,645	127,441	127,441
19	2,400	53,200	76,267	76,267	140,228	140,228
20	0	53,200	78,555	78,555	151,446	151,446
AGE 70	0	53,200	91,066	91,066	222,524	222,524

PROJECTED VALUES ARE BASED ON THE ILLUSTRATED CURRENT INTEREST RATE OF 8% IN THE FIRST POLICY YEAR AND 8% IN THE SUBSEQUENT YEARS.

those prescribed by the National Association of Securities Dealers (NASD) but you may project into the future. Not so with variable annuities since future projections may not be used.

ACCOUNT AND BALANCE SUMMARIES

Contract owners receive a flow of written communication beyond the usual sale confirmations and delivery of the policy. A summary of account activity and balances is sent, usually several times each year. The account activity includes: payments made since the last report, transfers in and out of the account, surrenders, and any fees charged to the account. The account balance section includes: the number of units held, the value of each unit, and the accumulation value (or contract value) in the account. A sample account activity summary appears in Figure 5.04.

Figure 5.04

ABC Life Insurance Company
100 Main Street
Washington, D.C. 20020

STATEMENT FOR: John Taylor
                     200 Jefferson St.
                     Washington, DC 20020

REPRESENTATIVE: Melissa Morgan, CLU

CONTRACT DATA

                    Owner: Taylor, John
                    Annuitant: Taylor, John
                    Contract Number: 123456ABC
                    Plan: Nonqualified
                    Contract Date: 1-1-93
                    Social Security Number: 123-45-6789

STATEMENT PERIOD: 12/31/96 to 06/03/97

CONTRACT ACTIVITY

Sub-Account Name	No. of Units as of 12/31/96	Unit Value as of 12/31/96	Dollar Value as of 12/31/96
Growth	455.529	33.167	15,108.88

Sub-Account Name	No. of Units as of 6/30/97	Unit Value as of 6/30/97	Dollar Value as of 6/30/97
Growth	455.529	36.756	16,743

CONTRACT SUMMARY

Beginning Annuity Value: $15,108.88
Total Payments: 0.00
Total Withdrawals: 0.00
Total Charges: 0.00
Ending Cash Value: $16,415.89
Ending Annuity Value: $16,743.61

PERIODIC REPORTS

Once each year, and sometimes more than once, a printed report is sent pertaining to the variable annuity in general and the fixed and variable accounts in particular. This report contains comments and information from the issuing company management and from certain of the investment advisors, general economic and investment information which may have an impact on the accounts and investors in them, and some performance data pertaining to the accounts. The report also contains specific listings of the investments held in each of the variable accounts as of the close of the previous reporting period.

PRODUCT FEATURES

Many of the features of the variable annuity contract can be considered marketing and sales support aids. Product features are taken up in detail in Chapter 7. For the time being consider the following list of product features which may be used in the sales process:

1.   The ease of allocating premiums to the various accounts and the ease of changing the allocation as desired. The allocation may be changed with a simple notification.

2.   The ease of making transfers among accounts, including such methods as telephone transfers; some transfer limitations may apply. Generally, a number of transfers may be made each year without fee, and even more with a modest fee.

3.   The ease of maintaining an asset allocation balance in the accounts, including the use of automatic rebalancing, if available. Even without automatic rebalancing, the ease of making transfers can maintain asset allocation balance.

4.   Dollar cost averaging among accounts, if available, as discussed above.

5.   The ease of making withdrawals from the contract, including the availability of periodic withdrawal plans which provide for systematic withdrawals as requested by the contract owner.

6.   The waiver of any remaining surrender charges for withdrawals requested when the annuitant is in a nursing home or terminally ill.

7.   The existence of a death benefit, a payment to a beneficiary which will never be less than a certain amount, no matter what the experience of the variable accounts.

8. The multitude of payout options available to the annuitant or to the annuitant and spouse (or other individuals) on either a fixed or variable basis. Nearly any arrangement can be accommodated, along with guarantees of payments to others when the annuitant does not live long enough.

We began this chapter with some statements about customer satisfaction and achieving it when the customer feels comfortable in taking action and feels that he/she is saving and investing in ways that are comfortable. The methods of attaining comfort in taking action mentioned here, as well as the publications and tools discussed, should go a long way in accomplishing a desirable level of customer satisfaction.

CHAPTER FOOTNOTES

1. Amy S. Friedman, "Managing Clients' Investment Outlook," *National Underwriter*, Life and Health/Financial Services edition, April 21, 1997, reporting on an address by Roger Gibson, president of Gibson Capital Management, Ltd., Pittsburgh, PA.

2. *Ibid.*

3. "Outlook from the SEC," *NAVA Outlook*, September/October, 1996.

6

LICENSING, COMPLIANCE AND ETHICS

REGISTERED PRODUCTS

Variable annuities are registered products. That is, they are registered with the Securities and Exchange Commission and governed by provisions of the securities laws of the United States and the states where the issuing companies are domiciled and operate.

The most prominent federal laws are the Securities Act of 1933, which regulates variable annuities and securities, and the Investment Company Act of 1940, which regulates them as periodic payment plans. Recently, the National Securities Markets Improvement Act of 1996 made changes affecting pricing as discussed in Chapter 8. Marketing and sales activities are regulated by the National Association of Securities Dealers (NASD), a self-regulatory organization.

Caution

State laws also regulate securities and securities marketing activities within their borders. And states have exclusive jurisdiction over the licensing of agents, the approval of insurance policies and contracts, and the marketing of insurance products (including annuities). In this context, a variable annuity is considered to be an insurance product. Thus, a sales representative who intends to market and sell variable annuities must be a licensed agent or sales representative in the state as well as a registered representative with the proper licenses and registrations as administered and supervised by securities authorities. The state requirements vary from state to state; generally, the requirements supervised on the federal level do not. A registered representative who wants to market and sell in more than one state must be mindful of the requirements of each of the states. His broker/dealer usually is in a position to make him/her aware of what is required.

BROKER/DEALER PRODUCTS ONLY

A registered representative must be associated with a broker/dealer whose duty it is to see that the representative is qualified as a sales person and to supervise his/her marketing and sales activities. The insurance company, with which the broker/dealer is affiliated, often takes responsibility for the licensing of the person as an agent; it often also assists the broker/dealer in administering its securities licensing activities. Since the representative often is licensed and contracted to sell other products of that company, this is a natural extension.

The registered representative may market only the products of the broker/dealer (in addition to the non-registered products of the company(s) with which he/she is associated). A broker/dealer may handle a great number of products, especially several families of mutual funds, but it may have only one or a few variable annuities available. Some of these may be products of other insurance companies with which the broker/dealer has selling arrangements. This means the sales representative may sell only that one or those few. This is a marked departure from the prevalent practice with respect to fixed annuities. Since fixed annuities are not registered products, it is common for many sales representatives to offer not only those products issued by their primary companies but those of other companies, with which they have brokerage affiliations.

Definition

Only a few years back, it was not uncommon for a registered representative to have dual registrations. That is, he/she was affiliated with more than one broker/dealer and was in a position to market products of any of them. The problem with dual registration is that a broker/dealer whose product is not the one being marketed often is held responsible, and therefore liable, for not adequately supervising the acts of a registered representative while marketing a product of another broker/dealer. This extension of risk has led many broker/dealers to no longer agree to dual registrations for representatives registered with them. As a result, dual registrations are much less common today.

There have been other related developments. Some broker/dealers have been cited for lack of adequate supervision in matters having to do primarily with the non-registered products being sold by their registered representatives. The findings have been based, in part, on the fact that the representatives were seen to be acting in the capacity of a registered representative though the products at issue were not registered. This is a troublesome development for broker/dealers which, heretofore, had concerned themselves only with the representative's conduct with respect to the products of the broker/dealer. For that reason, broker/dealer supervisory activities sometimes cross into areas not strictly having to do with registered products.

SECURITIES LICENSES

A number of different securities licenses may be required in order to sell different types of securities. Since some of them are required at the state level, there are variations.

1. For variable annuities, mutual funds, and variable life insurance, NASD Series 6, Investment Company/Variable Contract Products. This is the shortest route to licensing for variable annuities.

2. For limited partnerships, NASD Series 22, Direct Participation Programs. This license is needed to sell oil and gas programs, real estate and other limited partnerships.

3. For municipal bonds, etc., Municipal Securities Rulemaking Board (MSRB) Series 52, Municipal Securities. This license is needed to sell municipal and U.S. government and government agency securities.

4. For stocks and bonds, etc., NASD Series 62, Corporate Securities. In addition to stocks and bonds, this covers rights, warrants, closed-end funds, real estate investment trusts and other asset-backed securities.

5. For comprehensive securities licensing, NASD Series 7, General Securities. This license takes the place of the four preceding licenses and permits the license holder to sell all of these products.

6. For futures, NFA Series 3, Commodity Futures. This license is needed to sell agriculture, financial, government securities, and precious metals futures.

7. For state-level registration, North American Securities Administrators Association (NASAA) Series 63, Uniform Securities State Law Exam. This exam, which may be required in addition to one or more of those above, is needed in states requiring state-level registration.

8. For state-level registration as a registered investment adviser (RIA), NASAA Series 65, Uniform Investment Adviser Exam. This exam, which may be required in addition to any of those above, is needed in states requiring state-level registration as an RIA.

9. For combination state-level registration, NASAA Series 66, Uniform Combined State Law Exam. This exam combines material from both Series 63 and 65 and may be taken in place of them.

All of these examinations are of the multiple-choice variety and are taken on computer terminals in exam locations. The time permitted for taking the exams varies, of course, but most are in the range of 2 to 3 hours. There is one notable exception and that is Series 7, which permits 6 hours. In nearly all cases, a passing grade is 70 percent; in some cases, a passing score is needed in each of the major areas covered.

Frequently, it is debated as to whether one should "go the whole route" by taking Series 7 or take the other four exams one-at-a-time, preparing for each separately. There is no one answer. Some people are able to remember large amounts of information easier than others. Some are better off "biting off a little at a time." Some people will have an easier time "gearing up" for one big effort than exercising the necessary self-discipline to follow through with a series of examinations.

Sometimes, the point is made that a sales person should be knowledgeable on all of the types of product choices the customer may have. While this is a worthy goal it may be somewhat unrealistic. There can be little doubt that much of the information learned for an exam is soon forgotten if it is not used on some regular basis. Learning about the great variety of financial services products is a formidable job, one that requires continuous attention and effort long after examinations have been passed.

SUPERVISOR LICENSING

Those who supervise registered representatives, whether the representatives are engaged in sales or in administrative functions which require licensing, are required to also be licensed as principals (or sales supervisors in the case of General Securities registration). Following are the licenses available:

- NASD Series 4, Registered Options Principal

- NASD Series 8, General Securities Sales Supervisor

- NASD Series 24, General Securities Principal

- NASD Series 26, Investment Company/Variable Contracts Principal

- NASD Series 27, Financial and Operations Principal

- NASD Series 39, Direct Participation Program Principal

- MSRB Series 53, Municipal Securities Principal

These examinations, too, may be taken on computer terminals in exam centers. Similar time periods are permitted and a score of at least 70 percent is needed to pass.

State examinations for licensing as an insurance agent and additionally, if needed, to be able to sell variable annuities are administered in a variety of ways. Since a number of states now use examinations prepared by professional testing organizations, there is more standardization among the states than once was the case. Most examinations are multiple choice and a score of 70 or 75 percent is needed to pass. Besides examinations, there may be additional state filings and other requirements to qualify to sell securities in a particular state.

Caution

A sales representative's broker/dealer registration may terminate, because he/she has changed companies or because he/she is not doing the required quantity of business or because the representative has not paid applicable fees. The representative may remain unaffiliated with a broker/dealer for up to two years. After that, the representative must take the various tests anew in order to affiliate with a broker/dealer. For this reason, representatives are keen to make a new affiliation before the two year period has expired.

REGISTERED INVESTMENT ADVISOR

Many registered representatives who concentrate on advising customers about their financial affairs and about selecting financial services products choose to register themselves as registered investment advisers (RIA). In some states, one must be an RIA (or RIA associate) to charge fees for such activities as financial planning. Even when it is not required, some registered representatives will want to be in a position to inform their customers that they have this additional registration and the knowledge and supervision which go with it.

Definition

A registered investment adviser is registered with the Securities and Exchange Commission, which means his office is subject to inspection by the SEC. Additionally, an RIA is held to a higher standard of conduct. As we have seen, he/she must have passed the NASAA Series 65 or Series 66 exam and, in some states, must be registered with the state securities department, which also has the right to inspect his/her office. Some states also require that an RIA hold a Series 7 license. Obviously, RIA status is not to be taken lightly. Considerable responsibility, time and some added expense are involved.

An alternative to individual RIA status is that of being an RIA associate. A broker/dealer which is registered as an RIA may appoint certain of its registered representatives as RIA associates. Those appointed must pass the same exams, and be trained by the broker/dealer which remains responsible for supervision. There may be additional state filings required. But the RIA associate is in compliance with state laws regarding charging fees and similar matters.

COMPLIANCE MEETINGS

Reminder

The NASD requires broker/dealers to have their registered representatives attend annual compliance meetings. These are meetings where a major portion of the time is devoted to compliance matters and issues. Those attending are reminded of the rules of conduct, of potential pitfalls, and any new procedures are explained and implemented as needed.

Compliance meeting practices vary from one broker/dealer to the next. Some of the larger ones consider it up to the registered representative to take the opportunity to attend and expect their representatives to present themselves at one of the announced times and locations. Other broker/dealers take a more active role by having compliance officers and others conduct meetings in some of the affiliated offices. Nearby representatives also can attend.

As indicated, annual attendance is required by the NASD. The broker/dealer will be held responsible if a registered representative does not attend. For that reason, it is the broker/dealer which must impose any sanction on the registered representative. The most common sanction is suspension of the representative's ability to do business through the broker/dealer until he/she meets the compliance meeting requirement. Since suspension interrupts the flow of commissions on broker/dealer products, this sanction usually is effective.

CONTINUING EDUCATION

Since July, 1995, there have been two NASD requirements for continuing education. First, on the second, fifth and tenth anniversaries of their registrations, registered representatives must participate in computer-based updating sessions. Those participating are given 3½ hours to answer questions on pertinent information and procedures. Should they not be able to answer enough questions correctly in the allotted time, they must participate on subsequent occasions. Registered representatives who have been registered for ten years or longer are excused from this requirement under a "grandfather" provision.

Second, each broker/dealer must provide an annual continuing education program for all of its registered representatives. The broker/dealer is to formulate the content of this program based on an analysis of the needs of the broker/dealer and its representatives. A representative's registration is not at risk for failure to meet the continuing education requirements but the broker/dealer may need to suspend activity involving the representative until the requirements are completed.

SALES LITERATURE

The broker/dealer also is responsible for assuring that proper procedures are being followed in field sales offices and the use of sales literature and other procedures are in compliance. Many companies accomplish this by conducting inspections of field offices from time to time. The inspections usually are carried out by compliance personnel, during visits for other compliance activities, or by company sales management personnel in their compliance capacities.

Reminder

A registered representative may use only those sales materials approved by the broker/dealer. Most of the materials are either prepared by the issuing company or come from outside fund manager organizations and are approved by the broker/dealer.

Caution

Generally, sales materials are filed with the SEC for comment. The SEC's comments pertain to adequacy of disclosure for the most part. They may require additional information or suggest that certain wording be changed to improve disclosure. Note that the SEC does not "approve" the sales material as such. For that reason, it is not proper to say or imply that the sales material has been "approved by the SEC." Rather, the SEC has reviewed the material and has become satisfied that the level of disclosure in it is adequate. NASD rules of conduct also prohibit the use of sales material that is misleading. The broker/dealer is charged with enforcing these rules as it understands them.

Registered representatives may originate their own sales materials. Business cards and stationery must be printed as approved by the broker/dealer. Any advertisements or preapproach letters must be approved in advance of use. Most broker/dealers have sample advertisements and letters which have been approved and can be used as they are. About the only items that do not have to be approved in advance are individual communications with customers involving clerical and other matters not having to do with specific investment advice or the solicitation of business. Newspaper and magazine articles may be sent without approval as long as there are no comments added which can be seen as providing specific investment advice or soliciting business.

The fact of the matter is, issuing companies produce a great deal of good information which has been approved for distribution to the public. As long as so much of it is available, it seems unnecessary for registered representatives to go to the work of originating their own to any significant extent. Some representatives do write newsletters to send to their customers or to have published in customer publications. They also make articles produced by the issuing company available for publication. These newsletters and articles do not have to be approved so long as they contain only general investment information. Of course, the ones originated by issuing companies usually have been approved in any event.

DESIGNATED OFFICES

Definition

A broker/dealer may designate certain of its field offices as "branch offices." Generally, these are the larger offices which perform many of the sales functions that the broker/dealer would otherwise take care of. As branch offices, they are subject to inspection by the NASD and must conform to NASD rules. For example, the office files of investors must be kept apart from the files of those who purchase other products handled by the office.

Definition

Some very large broker/dealers will designate "offices of supervisory jurisdiction." These offices perform essentially all of the services of the broker/dealer and are subject to inspection by both the SEC and the NASD. Smaller broker/dealers generally will not have any offices of supervisory jurisdiction with all of the broker/dealer services performed at the same central location.

Reminder

There are a number of other sales practices governed by rules of conduct and broker/dealer and insurance company procedures. As discussed in Chapter 5, the variable annuity prospectus must be presented at or mailed in advance of the first contact with a potential customer when a variable annuity product is to be discussed. The prospectus is the primary disclosure publication and it must be available to the potential customer from the start.

Also as mentioned in Chapter 5, profiles, to accompany the prospectus, currently are being used on a trial basis. The profiles are simplified, compared to prospectuses, and easier for some potential customers to understand. The SEC hopes that the profiles can lead to simplified documents which can provide adequate disclosure so that prospectuses, as we now know them, can be replaced. Such a development is expected to take some time.

SUITABILITY STATEMENT

When a customer applies to purchase a variable annuity, the registered representative usually is required by the broker/dealer to complete a suitability statement. The NASD rule states that the registered representative "...shall make reasonable efforts to obtain information concerning: (1) the customer's financial status; (2) the customer's tax status; (3) the customer's investment objectives; and (4) such other information used or considered to be reasonable...in making recommendations to the customer."[1]

Questions for determining suitability usually are a part of the application, frequently found on the back or adjacent to it. Generally, the issuing company will not accept an application if the suitability portion has not been completed. Answers to the questions should lead to the conclusion that the variable annuity being applied for is a suitable investment for a person who has answered the questions as they have been answered.

Premiums paid by the potential customer must be credited to annuity accounts within five days following the day they were collected. For this reason, the application must specify what accounts the customer wants to use. When the allocation has not been made, the company may retain the money in an account, such as the money market account, temporarily but only with the express direction of the customer. Obviously, everyone is better off if the details of the allocation are settled by the time the application is sent to the issuing company for action. We should note here that the time requirement for funds settlement for variable annuities differs from that of stocks. Stock purchases must be made within three days following the collecting of purchase funds.

As discussed in Chapter 5, there are limitations on the use of sales illustrations of variable annuities. With respect to the guaranteed or fixed account, projections of interest rates into the future may be made using the current rate and the guaranteed rate. An assumed interest rate also may be used provided that the current and guaranteed rates also are shown. This is the same rule that applies to fixed annuities.

Reminder

On the contrary, no future projections involving the variable accounts may be shown. However, a portrayal of illustrative amounts of premium put into the variable accounts in the past, and remaining or continuing for ten years to today may be shown. These illustrations are instructive as to how the accounts operate but it is improper to imply that the situation will continue to be the same in the future. In fact, one must make a point of saying it is very unlikely to be the same.

That no future projections of variable accounts may be shown is a different rule from the one that applies to variable life and variable universal life insurance. With life insurance products, hypothetical interest projections into the future may be made. The rates which may be used are the ones prescribed by the NASD.

CONTRACT DELIVERY

A most important practice is for the registered representative to deliver the variable annuity contract promptly and obtain a delivery receipt. Generally, the contract provides that the owner will have a brief period of time, e.g., 10 days or 20 days, to examine it and, if he/she chooses, to return it for a full refund. This is the so-called "free look" provision. The free look period does not start to run until the contract is delivered; therefore, the delivery must be prompt.

The situation involving "free coverage" which arises when an insurance policy is not delivered promptly is serious enough. But when there are variable accounts involved, as is usually the case with a variable annuity, the situation is even more serious. After all, the value of the account(s) may diminish significantly before the free look period has ended. Issuing companies sometimes place the premiums in less volatile accounts temporarily awaiting the return of the delivery receipt and/ or running of the free look period. Some companies also withhold the crediting of new business, and payment of sales compensation, until the delivery receipt is received.

ETHICAL PRACTICES

The SEC and NASD, on the national level, and state insurance departments, on the state level, have devised the various compliance practices, procedures and tests to serve the public. They are designed to assure, to the extent possible, that there will be proper disclosure of pertinent information pertaining to financial services products, that the products will be suitable for people in particular circumstances, and that those with whom the public consults will be competent, knowledgeable and will follow good business practices. That is to say, the authorities are doing what they can to see that broker/dealers and their registered representatives engage in ethical conduct. Of course, there is more to good ethics than "crossing the T's and dotting the I's" with respect to licenses, sales literature, compliance meetings, and continuing education.

What someone does publicly often is not as important as what he/ she does in private. A person can attend all the classes, get all the licenses and registrations, and sign all of the suitability forms and statements of ethical conduct — the public things — but not do nearly so well in private. In other words, there are the attitudes the person has toward good ethics and there are the practices and habits the person actually maintains. It is said that though attitudes and values influence ethics, the clearest way to differentiate between highly ethical and unethical insurance professionals is to focus on their habits. Habits are the typical, conditioned approach people have for dealing with their professional conduct.[2]

CUSTOMER FOCUSED

The sales process of the highly ethical professional is customer focused. The needs of the customer are the first concern. Though we indicated in preceding chapters that a significant volume of sales is needed for most sales people to be successful selling financial services products such as variable annuities, this does not mean short cuts should be taken.

Caution

To be sure, shortcuts sometimes can be taken, but the ethical (and ultimately successful) sales representative will not take this route. One short cut in particular that should be avoided is to assume, with little investigation, that the customer knows exactly what he/she needs and that the task of the sales representative is to merely proclaim the virtues of the product he/she is selling. As we also have said earlier, because of all the publicity and financial reporting that has appeared, the customer may very well have a good idea of what he/she needs. But it is a mistake not to verify this assumption with solid fact finding and detailed analysis.

When your sales process is customer focused, you will gather fact finding information, analyze it, present your conclusions, determine what the customer's interests are, and present a product or products which serve those interests and provide answers to the needs ascertained. You will also want to educate your potential customer so that he/she knows what is being proposed and presumably purchased. There are a number of steps to this process but it does not necessarily have to extend over many meetings or consume a great deal of time. The potential customer may have come to some tentative conclusions which you will only need to verify.

Reminder

A highly ethical professional will engage in continuing education that is considerably in excess of that required to maintain licenses and registrations. There is constant change in financial services products, in financial markets, in interest rate markets, in the tax law, and in other laws affecting the registered representative's marketplace. One would never want to discuss a product with which he/she is not familiar. On the other hand, neither would one want to overlook a product which might be useful and the answer to one of the customer's needs. One would never want to be unaware of a tax or other law change which can impact a customer. As it is said, you must "sharpen your tools" regularly. Besides that, changes present perfect opportunities to contact customers so that you can offer additional services or bring up financial needs that had been discussed previously. Many things could have happened in the customer's life since your last discussion.

DOCUMENTATION

Highly ethical professionals are careful about making sure paperwork is in order. They keep copies of fact finding and other forms, such as asset allocations and similar items used in the sales process. They are careful to complete and have the customer sign all disclosure forms, retaining copies. It is required that many disclosure forms be given to customers for their records but it is not wise to depend on customers to retain them where they can be found.

Having good documentation can be of immense value if the customer claims, justified or not, that he/she has not been dealt with fairly, something more apt to happen when account values drop. Documentation can not only offer legal protection to you, the registered representative, if that becomes necessary but it can be used to refresh the customer's recollection of what transpired during the sales process, in the event he/she remembers things differently. The value of good documentation in deterring a potential problem often is more valuable than its legal value because, after all, you want to retain good customers not gather ammunition to fight them.

REMEMBER — VALUES CAN GO DOWN

Reminder

We must never fail to make it clear to customers that variable annuity values can go down as well as up. Great enthusiasm, sometimes rising to euphoria, takes place at the time of a sale. The sales representative is enthusiastic because his/her recommendations have been accepted and a sale has resulted. The customer is enthusiastic because he/she has done a most difficult thing — he/she has made a decision.

This enthusiasm can lead to a feeling that "nothing can go wrong." Whereas, it is assured that something will go wrong. Even if the customer's accounts do very well indeed, they may not do as well as the customer's hopes had projected them to do. And some of the customer's accounts can actually lose money, an unthinkable outcome. This is especially so in the short term. Again, remember that values can go down as well as up.

CHAPTER FOOTNOTES

1. NASD Conduct Rules, Rule 2310, "Recommendations to Customer (Suitability)." *National Association of Securities Dealers Manual.*

2. Dennis M. Groner, "The Habits of Highly Ethical Insurance Professionals," *National Underwriter,* Life and Health/Financial Services edition, March 31, 1997.

7

PRODUCT FEATURES AND CHARACTERISTICS

ANNUITY CLASSIFICATIONS

Annuities are traditionally classified in several ways:

1.   how premiums are paid;

2.   when the annuities are to mature;

3.   whether there is more than one annuitant;

4.   whether the annuities are fixed or variable; and

5.   whether the annuities are qualified or nonqualified.

There are other descriptive titles used in recent years as we will explore later in this chapter.

If classified according to premium, annuities are either single premium or periodic premium (which includes annual, semi-annual, quarterly and monthly). As to the maturity date, annuities are either immediate or deferred. An immediate annuity begins payouts at the end of the first payout period; that is, the first monthly payment occurs at the end of the first month after the annuity is purchased. In contrast, a deferred annuity does not begin payouts until some-time later.

Definition

Regarding the annuitant, which is the person whose life is used to measure the annuity payout periods, annuities are either single or joint. A single annuity has a single annuitant while a joint annuity has more than one.

Finally, annuities are either fixed or variable, as discussed earlier and either qualified or nonqualified. A qualified annuity is one used to fund a qualified retirement plan while a nonqualified annuity is not part of a qualified plan. Generally speaking, most variable annuities are periodic premium, deferred, single life annuities.

PREMIUMS

With a variable annuity contract, the issuing company must agree to accept the initial premium. This initial premium, when accepted with the application and any additional requirements, puts the contract in force. Subsequent premiums will be accepted automatically provided that the contract's minimum and maximum premium requirements are met. Companies are careful to see that compliance and suitability requirements have been met before accepting the first premium which must be applied to the accounts specified by the contract owner within five days, unless the owner has requested that it be held longer.

Typically, companies have minimum premium requirements for initial premiums and for subsequent premiums. Initial premiums may be relatively low, amounts such as $50, $100, $1,000, or $2,000. Or, they may be relatively high, amounts ranging from $5,000 to more than $25,000.

Subsequent premiums often can be and are less than the initial premium. Companies frequently have maximum premiums as well, which sometimes can be waived in accordance with the provisions contained in the prospectus.

The usual methods of paying premiums are used with variable annuities —annual, semi-annual, quarterly and monthly, especially by preauthorized check. Since most variable annuities have flexible premiums, meaning that they may vary at the will of the contract owner within the minimums and maximums, the premium notices are more on the order of reminder notices. The contract owner will make additional premium payments when he/she decides to do so.

Generally, companies reserve the right, when new premiums have not been paid for some period of time and the account values are minimal, to terminate the contract and return the values to the owner. Of course, contracts with high minimum initial premiums do not encounter this minimal account values situation unless there have been large withdrawals.

ISSUE AND MATURITY AGES

Variable annuities are issued to young and middle-aged persons as well as to individuals who are fairly well along in years, often up to the ages of 80, 85, or even 90. Immediate annuities, which begin paying out benefits right away, can be issued to nearly any age, providing that suitability requirements are met.

Most variable annuities have a maturity date which is the contract anniversary date upon which the annuitant reaches a certain age. Annuities used in Individual Retirement Arrangements and Tax Deferred Annuities (sometimes called Tax Sheltered Annuities) must begin distributions near the annuitant's age 70½. Annuities used in qualified retirement plans are governed by the terms of the plans which require payouts to begin at stated times.

Nonqualified annuities have maturity dates at higher ages, e.g. 75, 85, or 90. The reason for this is traditional; the thinking is that in order for an annuity to be considered an insurance and annuity product, it must not resemble too closely a security such as a mutual fund. One of the ways of distinguishing an annuity is the prominence of payout features. Therefore, there must be a discernible time when payouts will begin, a maturity date. Because people are living to older and older ages, the need for higher maturity ages is recognized. For that reason, some annuities today are rather vague about their maturity dates.

ACCUMULATION UNITS

Definition

When premiums are received, any applicable charges are deducted, and the balance is credited to the guaranteed or fixed interest account, if available, and to the variable accounts selected by the owner in the form of "accumulation units." Accumulation units are determined by dividing the amount allocated to each variable account by the accumulation unit value for that account. Thus, the premium allocated purchases a given number of units and fractions of a unit. The value of the accumulation units in the different accounts will vary in accordance with the investment experience of the account and the expenses charged to that account. The contract value (accumulation value or similar designation) of the variable annuity contract is the sum of the different variable accounts and the guaranteed account, if applicable.

Reminder

The value of the accumulation units in the variable accounts is expected to change frequently, and will depend on the investment performance and expenses of the portfolio in which the variable account invests. The value of the units is determined every day that the stock markets are open. It is determined at the close of business one day and then is determined next at the close of business on the following day. As we see, the variable annuity contract owner's contract value is derived from the value of the accumulation units and guaranteed account, not directly from the prices of the stocks and/or bonds held in the variable accounts. Although, it is true that the stocks and bonds provide the basis for calculating the accumulation units.

When the contract reaches the date at which annuity payments are to begin, the annuitant generally can have a fixed or a variable payout, or a combination of the two. The amount of variable payments is determined using a similar valuation method. These units sometimes are referred to as "annuity units." We will take up the various payout options later in this chapter.

VARIETY OF VARIABLE ACCOUNTS

A prominent feature of today's variable annuities is the large number and variety of variable accounts available for investing. In a recent listing of variable annuity contracts,[1] nearly all the contracts listed offered at least eight or ten variable accounts and a large number of the annuity contracts maintained at least fifteen or twenty variable accounts. Further, some annuity contracts offered variable accounts that ran into the upper thirties and even to forty. This is a great deal of variety, perhaps more than some potential annuity owners wish to deal with. But, no one can complain over a lack of choices.

Example

Each variable account is characterized by type and has a stated objective and investment policy or strategy. For example, a bond portfolio might be listed as an income or bond type. The objective might be to seek as high a level of current income as is consistent with reasonable investment risk, investing primarily in long-term, fixed-income, investment-grade corporate bonds. The investment policy or strategy might mention that at least seventy-five percent of the value of assets would be in publicly traded debt securities rated BBB or Baa or higher, or guaranteed by the government, etc.

In addition to a conventional bond portfolio, a variable annuity might offer other variable accounts similar to these:

1. Growth or equity – seeking long-term appreciation without incurring unduly high risk; investing in special opportunity securities that are selling at a discount from theoretical price/earnings ratios and seem capable of recovering.

2. Growth with income – seeking to provide reasonable current income and long-term growth of capital and income; investing at least 65 percent in common stock or convertibles that are believed to have long-term prospects for growth and income, including foreign securities.

3. Aggressive growth – seeking better-than-average capital growth; investing in common stocks and equity equivalents that meet certain fundamental and technical standards of selection and have better than average potential for appreciation.

4. Balanced or asset allocation – seeking high total returns by investing in equity securities, debt instruments and money

market instruments; proportion of types of securities determined by the advisor based on value analysis, analysis of historical long-term returns, and other market influencing factors.

5. High yield – seeking high current income by investing primarily in a diversified portfolio of fixed income securities; investing in those fixed income securities, including lower rated bonds, which offer a current yield above that generally available on debt securities in the three highest rating categories.

6. International – seeking long-term growth of capital principally from a diversified portfolio of foreign equity securities; investing primarily in equity securities of established companies, listed on foreign exchanges, which the advisor believes have favorable characteristics.

7. Money market – seeking stability and current income from a portfolio of market instruments with an average maturity of 90 days; investing in money market securities such as U.S. Treasury, finance company and corporate commercial paper, domestic and foreign certificates of deposit, and corporate obligations.

8. Small company or small capitalization – seeking high long-term growth primarily from younger, small-to-midsize capitalization companies; investing at least eighty percent in common stocks of small and medium-size companies, which have just begun in their life cycles but have the potential to become major enterprises.

9. Specialty portfolios – investing in particular portfolios of investments such as those having to do with natural resources, utilities, precious metals, real estate, government securities, etc.

10. Equity – indexed accounts; interest crediting based in part on increases in an external equity index (see the discussion of equity-indexed annuities in this chapter).

This list is not intended to be complete but just to present some examples. Further, the listings themselves have been abbreviated. Those actually found in prospectuses and in sales materials usually are longer and provide more details. When variable annuity contracts have fifteen or twenty variable account choices, there usually is more than one of a particular category. Since accounts with similar objectives and investment policies or strategies own different investments, have encountered different performance results, and have employed different managers, there can be reasons for selecting one over another, even though the characteristics of the accounts appear similar.

The popularity of particular types of accounts changes from quarter to quarter and year to year as the investment market changes. According to *The VARDS Report*,[2] assets in the various types of variable accounts stood at the following percentages at the end of 1996:

1.	Growth	28.22%
2.	Growth and Income	9.11%
3.	All Other Equity Funds	14.04%
4.	Balanced/Asset Allocation	10.04%
5.	Corporate Bond High Quality	1.26%
6.	All Other General Fixed Income	4.40%
7.	Money Market	2.82%

The remainder of the assets were in guaranteed or fixed interest accounts. (See the following discussion.)

CHOICES POPULAR

The large number of choices available is appealing to potential customers. While they sometimes can find themselves confused by all of the choices, they usually can find at least a few that they like in particular; and since they can make changes virtually any time they like, they should not be put off by the array of choices. Among the many choices are some being managed by outside money managers; that is, money managers who are not directly associated with the company issuing the annuity are managing some of the portfolios. Although companies prefer that their own, proprietary funds be used as much as possible, since they make more money from those funds, they are happy to provide outside managed funds in order to increase the appeal of their variable annuities to potential customers.

Many of the outside funds are managed by companies with high levels of name recognition, most often because of performance records, news articles, and publicity surrounding their mutual funds. This is even more appealing to buyers.

In the course of this discussion, it must be noted that it is not possible to place an existing mutual fund in a variable annuity. In other words, if the ABC Mutual Fund has produced high returns and seems a desirable place to invest money neither a variable annuity contract owner nor the issuing company may make the ABC Mutual Fund a variable account of the variable annuity. However, a portfolio with many of the same characteristics as a mutual fund, like the ABC fund, often called a "clone" may be one of the variable annuity's variable accounts. Note, however, that for this tactic to be appropriate, the mutual fund must share the variable annuity's long-term objectives including accumulation for the retirement years. Further, it is not proper to imply that a particular mutual fund and a variable account are similar unless, in truth, they are similar. The fact that they are from the same companies, have the same objectives, and use some of the same money managers may not be enough.

GUARANTEED ACCOUNTS

Most variable annuities have guaranteed accounts (also called fixed interest, general or deposit accounts); these are similar in most significant respects to fixed annuities, except that money in them can be allocated to variable accounts while remaining within the variable annuity.

Often, there is a limit on how much may be reallocated from the guaranteed account at any one time or during a year. For example, the limit may be ten percent in any one year. There also may be a limit, such as ten percent, on the amount that can be reallocated to the guaranteed account. The reason for such limitations is that the issuing company has made investments, usually corporate and government bonds and similar instruments, with maturity dates of several years or longer into the future, in order to be able to pay the promised rate of interest on the funds in the guaranteed account. Shorter maturities would have rates too low to earn enough to pay the promised rate. The issuing company has had to factor in the knowledge that, for example, as interest is paid on the bonds it is buying for the guaranteed account, the interest being earned will have to be invested at going rates, rather than at the rates the bonds are earning. It cannot afford to also sell the bonds ahead of maturity at a probable discount. Therefore, most of the funds must remain in the guaranteed account.

The usual practice is for the current interest rate on money placed in the guaranteed account to be guaranteed for a period of at least one year. One year is a common current interest guarantee; other common ones are three years and five years. But practices include nearly any period from 30 days to seven years or longer. Once the initial period has run, renewal rates apply. Renewal rates can be for multi-year periods as well but it is more common for them to be renewed for one year at a time. Since the underlying investments for the initial period and for the successive renewal periods will vary as interest rate markets change, initial rates and renewal rates are apt to be different. In fact, an initial premium paid one month may have a different declared current rate than an initial premium paid in the next month.

Companies review current declared interest rates frequently, even if they change them rather infrequently. When changes are made, the new rates usually take effect rather quickly, within a few days or a week or so. There are times when market interest rates are quite volatile and other times when they are rather stable. To remain competitive in the guaranteed account, it is necessary that rates rise when market rates rise; it also is necessary for rates to fall when market rates fall. It does not take long to attract a good bit of money when the company's rate is out of line on the high side. And because of the current interest guarantee period, it may take a while to recover from such a situation.

When discussing the guaranteed account, one other application of the word "guarantee" is very important. It is the minimum interest guarantee. The variable annuity contract states that no less than a certain rate, generally in the three to four percent range, will be paid on funds in the account. There is no other performance guarantee in the variable annuity contract and none whatsoever with many other types of investments. When the volatility of markets affecting the variable accounts make variable annuity owners uncomfortable enough to want to "pull in their horns," the guaranteed account awaits them, to the extent transfers into it are permitted.

Guaranteed accounts always have been popular with variable annuity buyers. During the high interest days of the early 1990's, assets in those accounts were at or near 50 percent of the total assets held in variable accounts.[3] During the more recent unprecedented stock market rise, guaranteed account assets percentages reduced through the 40's and 30's to 30.11 percent by the end of 1996. Still, 30 percent is significant in pointing out the importance of having this guaranteed account available. And when it is time to move back into variable accounts, transfers may be made to the extent permitted.

ALLOCATION TO ACCOUNTS

When someone purchases a variable annuity, he/she must select which of the available accounts to use and indicate how much premium is to go into each. This allocation of premium will continue until the owner changes it, which may be done essentially at any time. The variable annuity buyer makes the selection on his/her own or with the advice of the registered representative, financial planner or other financial advisor.

Since the issuing company must place the money in accounts right away, the selection must be made at the time the application is submitted or immediately thereafter. In Chapter 5, we discussed asset allocation programs. Using information supplied by the buyer concerning personal circumstances, financial goals, and investment risk tolerance, these programs calculate an asset allocation model which they state should be viewed as broad guidelines on how to invest. The portfolios identified may be descriptive of variable accounts and the guaranteed account but usually are not the accounts themselves. Thus, the variable annuity buyer must do some translating into those accounts from which he/she is able to choose. And since the asset allocation model is intended as a guideline, the buyer may accept as much or as little of it as he/she deems appropriate.

TRANSFERS AMONG ACCOUNTS

Planning Tips

As has been mentioned numerous times, a big advantage to variable annuities is the fact that the owner can transfer funds among the various accounts. He/she might want to make transfers in order to change the mix of investments or to maintain the mix of investments originally selected in light of the fact that each of the accounts has performed differently from the others. Transfers among accounts are handled in a variety of ways.[4] However, the current trend is for there to be a certain number of free transfers permitted, e.g., six or twelve per year, with a fee, e.g., $10 or $20 applicable to additional transfers. Companies also have minimum amounts, e.g., $100, $300, $500, which may be transferred in a transfer transaction. Most people agree that this limited number of free transfers gives enough latitude to satisfy most variable annuity buyers and that those who want to engage in more active transferring ought to pay a little extra for the additional record keeping and handling.

AUTOMATIC REBALANCING

Some people believe that keeping the investment mix as the buyer intended is so important that there should be a mechanism for doing so without having to depend on the buyer to check his/her statement regularly and make transfers from some accounts to others. It is for that reason that automatic rebalancing was introduced not long ago.

Definition

With automatic rebalancing, the variable annuity owner directs that, until further notice, the company will maintain the present balance of assets by means of periodic transfers from one account to another. Practices vary on how frequently the rebalancing may take place, e.g., monthly, quarterly, yearly. Some minimum total balance, e.g., $5,000, in the variable annuity usually is required and other distribution or payout plans may not be available while the automatic rebalancing is in effect. Only those accounts in which the buyer is participating are included and it may be that only the variable accounts may be included in the program. As indicated, automatic rebalancing is relatively new and not all companies offer it.

As with many other things having to do with investing, not everyone thinks rebalancing is a good idea. Those opposed argue that by having the automatic system in effect, the buyer "stunts the growth" of an account which otherwise would climb to a considerable height by taking away from it, periodically, and transferring to other accounts. This might happen, of course, but the variable annuity owner can prevent it from going on for very long simply by directing that automatic rebalancing be discontinued. It can always be resumed later.

DOLLAR COST AVERAGING AMONG ACCOUNTS

Dollar cost averaging was discussed in Chapter 5. The principle is that investing regularly, as the prices of investments fluctuate up and down, has proven to be a good long-term strategy. When prices are lower, more shares are purchased; when they are higher, fewer shares are bought. Assuming a reasonable performance over the period by the security, the overall value will be greater than most people can achieve by picking when to invest and when not to invest (timing the market).

Some variable annuities offer dollar cost averaging with money already inside the contract. The buyer may authorize that periodically, e.g., monthly, the company will take a predetermined dollar amount, usually with a minimum, e.g., $100, and transfer it from one account, e.g., the money market account, to the other variable accounts in which the buyer is participating. This will take place until all of the money in the first account has been transferred. If the buyer continues to allocate ongoing premiums into the first account, the dollar cost averaging will continue, although the buyer can accomplish much the same thing by allocating to accounts on his/her own.

DEATH BENEFIT

A unique feature of variable annuities, as compared with mutual funds or individual securities, is the variable annuity death benefit applicable while the annuity is in the accumulation phase and has not matured. (The term, death benefit, should not be confused with its use as the major component of a life insurance policy.) The traditional death benefit, which is paid to the designated beneficiary of the variable annuity, is the amount of premiums paid (less any surrenders and applicable surrender charges) or the annuity's contract value, accumulated value, account value, etc., (all refer to the same figure) whichever is greater. As a result, the beneficiary will receive whatever the annuity is worth unless its value has dropped below the amount of net premiums paid, in which case the beneficiary gets the net premiums paid. There is no risk of getting less than the amount invested in the annuity.

Definition

It has occurred to a number of people that once the contract value of an annuity has increased to a substantial level above the net amount of premiums paid, it would be indeed unfortunate if a rapid downturn took place just before the death benefit is to be paid. While the beneficiary still could have what is promised, it could have been so much more. This situation has led to a multitude of methods of enhancing or stepping up death benefits.[5] Many of these methods guarantee that beneficiaries will receive no less than the contract value at stated earlier contract anniversaries. Many reset these figures, higher or lower, at stated intervals, e.g., every three, five, or six years. Others build in a percentage increase, e.g., three or four percent, as a floor. Many, if not most, variable annuities provide that once an annuitant reaches an advanced age, e.g., 75 or 85, death benefits are calculated differently.

SURRENDER CHARGES

Surrender charges are made against surrenders or withdrawals from the contract value of most variable annuities for a period of time. The surrender charge (sometimes referred to as a "backload") is used in pricing instead of an initial charge against the premium (referred to as a "frontload"). In nearly all products, it is applicable to values derived from each premium for a certain number of years, e.g., 5, 7, 9, but the rate declines each year. It might start at 5, 7 or 9 percent and reduce by one percent each year, for example. There is further discussion of charges and fees in the next chapter. Withdrawals from the guaranteed account sometimes are subject to a market value adjustment which is discussed briefly later in this chapter.

CHARGE-FREE WITHDRAWALS

When the annuity owner makes a partial surrender or withdrawal, surrender charges apply until they have run their course except that most contracts provide for surrender-charge-free withdrawals of some sort. The most common withdrawal provisions are those which provide that 10 percent, or sometimes 15 percent, of the contract value may be withdrawn in a contract year. The number of transactions in the year often is limited too.

Another common provision is one that permits a percentage, such as 10 percent, or the interest and earnings in that year, whichever is greater to be withdrawn without surrender charges. In a minority of cases, the withdrawal provision is cumulative. That is, the annual percentage amounts may be accumulated for a limited number of years and the sum of the percentages withdrawn without surrender charges. Cumulative withdrawal provisions can more easily be applied to variable accounts than to the guaranteed account for the same reasons as those limiting transfers from the guaranteed account to variable accounts as discussed above.

The surrender charge provisions applicable to withdrawals from the contract values are apart from any tax penalties which may apply for premature distributions. Unless the annuitant is age 59½ or one of the other exceptions applies,[6] 10 percent of the amount subject to tax is payable as a penalty along with the regular income tax otherwise payable.

PERIODIC WITHDRAWAL PROGRAM

A number of companies offer a periodic withdrawal program which is not one of the payout options. Under this type of program, the variable annuity owner may preauthorize withdrawals of a level amount of money or a percentage of the contract value each month, quarter, half-year or year. The arrangement may be discontinued any time. The withdrawals that are made may or may not be subject to surrender charges, depending on whether they fall within the surrender-charge-free amount permitted. If surrender charges are no longer applicable, there is no limit to the amount which may be withdrawn, except for any minimums or maximums applicable to the withdrawal program itself. Since a payout provision is not being employed, the income tax consequences, including any premature distribution penalties, of the withdrawal program are the same as those applicable to individual, non-programmed withdrawals. The program is especially useful for the individual, over age 59½, who wants to take withdrawals on a systematic basis prior to the time of turning to a payout option.

WAIVING SURRENDER CHARGES

Many variable annuities have provisions which waive surrender charges on surrenders or withdrawals under extreme conditions. The two most common conditions are when the owner is confined to an institution such as a nursing home and when the owner contracts a terminal illness. Under the first, the owner must have been confined for a certain length of time, e.g., 30 consecutive days, in an institution providing daily medical treatment, including certain nursing home facilities. Under the second, the owner must have contracted a condition which a physician states should result in death within twelve months. These provisions allow access to the contract values of the annuity without concern for surrender charges. This access can be of considerable benefit to the owner in paying for the expenses involved with the confinement or terminal illness.

Caution

It must be noted here that the fact that the annuity owner qualifies for a waiver of surrender charges under the terms of his/her annuity contract does not necessarily mean that he/she qualifies for the "disability" exception[7] to the 10 percent premature distribution tax. The applicable disability definition is the one in the Internal Revenue Code. That is, the individual must be "...unable to engage in any substantial gainful activity by reason of any medically determinable physical or mental impairment which can be expected to result in death or to be of long-continued and indefinite duration."[8]

In this chapter, we have discussed a number of the provisions contained in annuity contracts. As we have seen, there are a number of variations with respect to them. While it might be natural to assume that the best annuity contract is the one that has the most features and choices, this is not necessarily the case. There is a cost connected with most of the choices as we will discuss in more detail in the next chapter. Some are more evident than others. Sometimes, it is possible only to determine that the costs of a particular contract are relatively high on an overall basis. In any event, it usually is necessary to weigh features and options against costs and then attempt to determine how useful some may be to potential customers in light of the costs connected with them.

PAYOUT OPTIONS

When an annuity contract reaches its maturity date, it is time to make use of one or more of the many payout provisions. Payout provisions also may be implemented, at the annuity owner's request, prior to the maturity date. Payouts may be fixed or variable. We will discuss the options here in terms of fixed payouts. Fixed options usually are placed in the contract using factors for determining amounts. The factors are guaranteed which, taken together with the guarantees being provided in the annuity, are an advantage of annuities over some other financial services products. The owner may use the factors in the contract or alternate ones, based on current interest being paid by the company. Though most options involve a life income, two do not. Those two are the fixed amount and the fixed period payout options. The other payout options involve payments for life, or life contingencies, although some elements of fixed amount and fixed period options are sometimes involved as well.

Fixed Amount Payout Option

With this option, the amount of the benefit payment is decided upon and the period of time over which this set benefit amount will be paid is calculated using the contract value of the annuity, or a portion of it, and interest. The benefit amount may be paid on either a monthly, quarterly, semi-annual or annual payment basis. When the designated amount has been paid for the period calculated, all of the contract value used in the calculation, together with interest, will have been paid out. With a given contract value, the larger the fixed amount, the shorter the period of time over which payments will be made.

Fixed Period Payout Option

This is similar to the fixed amount option except it is the period of time that is known and the monthly, quarterly, semi-annual, or annual amount which must be calculated, using the contract value, or portion of it, and interest. When the calculated amount has been paid for the period designated, all of the contract value used in the calculation, together with interest, will have been paid out. With a given contract value, the longer the period of time selected, the less each payment will be over the period.

Life Annuity Payout Option

With this option, also known as the life income without refund, a monthly, quarterly, semi-annual or annual income for life is calculated, using the contract value, or a portion of it, and interest. The calculation uses annuity tables which indicate the probabilities of living for years into the future. The annuitant's age is used in the calculation, as is his/her sex unless a unisex table is used. The older the age, the higher the payment. Because females live longer than males payments to males of the same age are higher than those made to females.

The amount calculated will be paid as long as the annuitant lives. If he/she lives for three years, the amount paid out will be less than the contract value and interest from which payments were calculated. If the annuitant lives for 30 or 40 years, the amount paid out will likely be far more than the contract value, plus interest. If someone, in his/her mid to late 60's, wants to have the highest income possible for life, and dependents and children are otherwise provided for, this option is the one to use. It pays the most but when the annuitant dies, no payments are made to others.

Life Income with Period Certain Payout Option

Example

This option combines a life annuity with a fixed period option. An income is paid for the life of the annuitant, with the further provision that if the annuitant dies before a fixed period or period certain, e.g., 5, 10, 20 years, has been completed, payments will continue to a beneficiary for the balance of the period certain. For example, if the annuitant dies after three years, payments continue to a beneficiary for seven more years, when a ten year period certain has been selected. However, if the same annuitant lives for twelve years, no payments are made to the beneficiary since the annuitant received payments for the ten year certain period during his/her life. The amount of income for life is calculated in the same way, except that the factors used include not only the probabilities of living and interest, but the cost of providing the period certain. Thus, the life income to be paid will be higher if a ten year period certain is selected than if a twenty year period certain is used.

Life Income with Refund Payout Option

This is a variation on the life income with period certain option. In this case, an income is paid for the life of the annuitant, but if he/she dies after only a few years, payments will continue until all of the original contract value, usually not including the interest used in the calculation, is paid to a beneficiary. The refund is paid in the same installments as those being paid while the annuitant was alive, although the beneficiary may be permitted to take a discounted amount in a lump sum.

Joint and Survivor Annuity Payout Option

Under this option, a monthly, quarterly, semi-annual or annual income for the life of two (sometimes more) annuitants is calculated using the contract values, or a portion of them, and interest. Payments continue as long as either (or any) of the annuitants is living. The calculation takes into account the probabilities of both and either of the annuitants living for years into the future. The same age and sex considerations apply. This payout option is also known as a joint and survivor annuity without refund payout option.

Of note is the amount of the payment that continues following the death of the first annuitant. It may be the same amount, an arrangement referred to as joint and full or 100 percent survivor annuity. It may be half as much as when both annuitants were receiving the payout, called a joint and half or 50 percent survivor annuity. Or it may be two-thirds the amount being paid before, a joint and two-thirds survivor annuity. Naturally, the size of the payment while both annuitants are alive is affected by the percentage that will be paid to the survivor.

Joint and Survivor with Period Certain Payout Option

Here again, a life annuity, this time a joint and survivor annuity, is being combined with a fixed period option. The income being paid to the annuitants will operate as before, with the further provision that should both annuitants die within a short period of time, e.g., three years, payments will continue to a beneficiary for the balance of the period certain.

Changing the Payout Option

When a payout option has been selected, it may or may not be possible to make changes once the payments have begun. It sometimes is possible to end a fixed period or fixed amount option and take the remaining proceeds, after a discount for lost interest, in a lump sum. This is referred to as commuting the proceeds. This type of procedure is not so common with life income options. The reason is that the principles of pooled risks and averages operate so that some annuitants will live longer than expected and some will live for less time. To allow annuitants to change their minds after the payout period has started defeats the principle. For that reason, life annuitants frequently must stick with the arrangements they have made. On the other hand, some annuities provide for a limited amount of "mind changing" so long as the changes are not adverse to the interests of the group of annuitants as a whole.

VARIABLE PAYOUTS

The fact that circumstances change during an annuitant's payout years, especially the costs of the goods and services he/she must buy, is one of the reasons for the popularity of variable payouts. The beginning calculation of a variable payout option begins with an assumed rate of interest being used much in the same way as with the fixed options discussed above. Then, subsequent amounts are calculated using the performance of the variable accounts into which the buyer has allocated his/her premiums. Payout amounts usually are recalculated annually with the same amount being paid each period during the next year. If variable accounts appreciate in value, the payments increase; if the accounts depreciate, the payments decrease. There is no floor to the variable payout but most people think it unlikely that all of the variable accounts will falter at the same time.

IMMEDIATE VARIABLE ANNUITIES

Planning Tips

Some variable annuities are referred to as immediate variable annuities. For the most part, these operate the same as those described above, except that they are of the single premium variety, do not accept additional premiums, and begin paying out benefits right away. Immediate variable annuities are particularly useful when customers have received large amounts of money, as discussed in Chapter 2. When a variable annuity is designed for single premium, immediate payout applications only, it is possible to make some pricing adjustments, including those affected by the cost of features otherwise available during a period of accumulation. It also may be easier to provide for changes once the annuity payouts have begun.

PAYMENTS TO IMPAIRED RISKS

Definition

As discussed above, the payout rates for annuities are calculated using annuity tables. On the other hand, the cost of life insurance is calculated using a mortality table. A mortality table tracks the number of people who die each year while an annuity table tracks the number of people who remain alive each year. The individuals whose lives are being measured by annuity tables generally live longer than those being measured by mortality tables because they are different groups of people. People buy annuities assuming they will live a long time. They buy life insurance assuming they will die someday.

People whose health is such that they do not expect to live a normal lifespan still can benefit from buying variable annuities. They can have tax deferral, professional money management, a wide range of choices, guaranteed accounts, and most of the features discussed in this chapter. However, they probably should not elect life income payouts. They can take systematic withdrawals of the contract values. There are some annuity contracts designed especially for impaired risks and there also are products for the structured settlement market. Those who are being compensated for injuries over many years often have shortened lifespans. A payout option providing for an income for life would calculate periodic payments with variations from the standard life expectancy for persons of the same age.

MARKET VALUE ADJUSTMENT

Earlier, we referred to the fact that the guaranteed account in a variable annuity may be subject to a market value adjustment, although this provision more often is used with group annuities which also have variable accounts or separate accounts. Individual annuities with market adjustments more often are fixed annuities. A market value adjustment annuity provides an interest guarantee for a year or several years. Once the period has elapsed, for a brief period of time, e.g., 30 days, withdrawals may be made without any reduction or charge. Then, when a renewal interest rate guarantee takes effect, the market value adjustment provision is applicable for the new period.

Definition

The market value adjustment is a charge against the withdrawal based on a ratio of the current rates in interest rate markets and the rate guaranteed in the annuity. The adjustment is occasioned by the need for the company to sell securities backing the interest guarantee at a discount in order to have the cash for the withdrawal. Selling at a discount will be needed when the interest rate on the underlying securities is lower than current market rates. It is when market rates are higher than the rate in the annuity that annuity owners have incentive to make withdrawals in order to invest the money elsewhere. When the annuity provides for a market value adjustment, the contract relies less, if at all, on surrender charges on withdrawals in the early years following payment of the premiums.

EQUITY-INDEXED ANNUITY

A product which closely resembles a variable annuity but usually is considered to be a fixed annuity is the equity-indexed annuity, a new development in recent years. The premium that an equity-indexed annuity buyer pays is credited with interest on the basis of participating in increases (but not necessarily decreases) in an external equity index, e.g., the S & P 500 Index.

The buyer may also have the option of directing a portion of his/her premium to what is otherwise a standard fixed annuity with an interest rate guarantee. The rate of participation of money placed in the equity-indexed annuity or portion will vary from time to time. To illustrate, let us use the example of $100,000 being placed in the equity-indexed portion.

Example

S & P 500 Index at start of index period	500
S & P 500 Index at end of index period	570
Index gain	14%
Participation rate	80%
Equity index gain	11.2%
Interest to be credited (on $100,000)	$11,200

The increase in the S & P index from the start of the period to the end of the period is 70 points, a gain of 14%. Since the equity-indexed annuity has a participation rate of 80%, the annuity will be credited with an interest rate of 11.2% which is arrived at by taking 80% of 14%. Thus, the equity-indexed portion begins the next period with $111,200; as a result, if the S & P 500 Index showed a loss during the following period, the equity-indexed portion would still have $111,200, at least until the next adjustment date. This ratcheting of increases is in some contracts and not others but in the latter cases, the original premium amount may be guaranteed.

Participation rates can range from 75 percent to over 100 percent; there are a number of contracts with exactly 100 percent. There are several ways of determining the index change. The simplest measures the growth from the first day of the index period (usually one year) to the last day. Another measures the growth from the first day to an average of the final three to six months.

Equity-indexed annuities often have surrender charges for early withdrawals as well as limited withdrawals without surrender charges. There usually are minimum cash value guarantees which apply to the equity-indexed portion as well as the guaranteed portion. Most have waiver of surrender charges in the event of terminal illness, confinement in a nursing home, or death. When the contract has both a guaranteed portion and an equity-indexed portion, transfers of existing values from one to the other are permitted with some limitations on amounts or percentages and/or timing of transfers.

Most equity-indexed annuities are being designed in the hope that their features will not cause them to be seen as securities and, therefore, subject to registration requirements. The reason is that, as non-registered products, they can be offered to many more distribution outlets. There are those who think that the index-linked interest crediting mechanism, which results in the annuity owner not knowing the return on the annuity until the end of the index period, makes the product similar to a mutual fund and not within the "safe harbor" of Securities and

Caution

Exchange Commission Rule 151.[9] Others disagree and say these products fall within the provisions of the rule.

SEC Rule 151 provides that a contract must meet three conditions to be within the "safe harbor":

1.   The contract is issued by a corporation (an insurance company) subject to the supervision of a state insurance commissioner.

2.   The insurer assumes a prescribed investment risk under the contract.

3.   The contract is not marketed primarily as an investment.

Equity-indexed annuities offer some of the "up side" of investing without much of the "down side," an arrangement that will be appealing to many annuity buyers. It may be that as more and more of these products come onto the scene, with more and more features and approaches, they may eventually be viewed as securities.

Of course, those who market variable annuities will be able to take such a development in stride. They already have the necessary registrations and licenses. It should not take their broker/dealers long to acquire the ability to market one or more equity-based annuities. In fact, those marketing variable annuities may already be marketing the equity-indexed products their broker/dealers will make available because the insurance company and broker/dealer are associated.

GROUP ANNUITIES

Most of the product information discussed in this chapter describing individual variable annuities also applies to group variable annuities, more often called group annuities with separate accounts. The biggest use of group annuities is in qualified retirement plans where, generally, securities registration is not required because the annuities are not being marketed to individuals and because the characteristics and restrictions of qualified plans offer much of the consumer protection that registration would have provided. The buyers of the group annuities are the plan sponsors/employers or associations. Individual participants deal with their plan sponsors and are issued certificates of participation.

Planning Tips

The pricing of group annuities may include more variations in loads and charges as well as in available compensation arrangements. A question which always arises is whether to use group annuities with separate accounts or individual variable annuities when either can be used, such as in qualified plans. A rule of thumb many use is that the breakpoint is at about fifteen participants. With fewer people covered, individual products may be the correct approach; with more people, group annuities may be preferable. Of course, factors other than number of participants may need to be taken into consideration.

DEVELOPING NEW PRODUCTS

New annuity products and features are introduced nearly every day. There is always excitement and interest when something new comes along. Sometimes, there also is a period required for marketers to learn about the new offerings and to visualize how they will fit into the marketers' plans and operations. It is said that a product has an average "shelf life" of three to five years. During that time, built in changes, such as interest rate declarations, help maintain interest. Other relatively small changes, such as adding additional variable accounts or changing money managers of the accounts already included, and adding minor improvements help maintain marketing momentum.

Eventually, so much will have transpired in the marketplace that a new product must be developed and introduced. However, issuers of annuities always must remember that they must continue to provide service for products marketed in the past and cannot announce that "parts are no longer available for this item," as it is possible to do with many non-financial products. Today, much of the service can be provided only when sophisticated and easily accessed data processing is at hand and available widely. In order to know when it is necessary to make substantial changes or to develop a new product and gain some idea of what needs to be developed, actuaries do a trend analysis. Generally, it takes about three years of data for an effective analysis.

CHAPTER FOOTNOTES

1. Kosnett, Jeffrey R., "The Year In Annuities," *Life Association News*, December, 1996.

2. "Special Report, Year-End (12/31/96) Sales and Asset Survey", *The Variable Annuity Research and Data Service (VARDS)*, Financial Planning Resources, Inc.

3. *Ibid.*

4. Kosnett, Jeffrey R., "The Year In Annuities," *Life Association News*, December, 1996.

5. *Ibid.*

6. IRC Section 72(q)(2).

7. *Ibid.*

8.   IRC Section 72(m)(7).

9.   SEC Rule 151 adopted by SEC Release No. 33-6645, May 29, 1986. Annuity contracts which meet the Rule 151 safe harbor provisions fall within Section 3(a)(8) of the Securities Act of 1933 which exempts the contracts from the provisions of the 1933 Act.

8

CHARGES AND FEES: PRICING

GOOD VALUE, ADEQUATE RETURN

A variable annuity product must provide good value to the customer while providing an adequate return to the issuing company. Leaving aside the performance of the variable accounts, customer value arises when the charges and fees are low enough that their effect on account values is slight; but they must be high enough that the company is able to provide the services that the customer needs.

The challenge in managing a profitable variable annuity is ensuring that fees collected exceed expenses and other obligations by a certain margin. Establishing the fees and charges for a product is a significant part of pricing. A profitable variable annuity also depends on critical mass; there must be adequate assets over which to spread the fixed costs.[1] This means there must be sufficient sales and, further, that those who purchase must remain contract owners to provide cash flow to the issuing company.

Naturally, in addition to being adequate, the charges and fees must be competitive with other variable annuity products, and, to a lesser extent, competitive with the charges and fees priced into mutual funds. However, in the case of mutual funds, an argument can be made that direct comparisons between variable annuities and mutual funds should be avoided because there are enough differences in the products and how they are used that such comparisons "muddy the water" and lead to more confusion than anything else. This subject is discussed more in Chapter 10.

Variable annuity issuers, of necessity, must be mindful of how competitive their products are in comparison to other variable annuities. Registered representatives and buyers are interested as well. Looking at rankings, of one kind and another, can be helpful but there often is more to the story. Since the charges and fees charged to the variable accounts are reflected in their performance figures, performance rankings might be used. But the fact is, the performance may have more to do with the selection of the investments, the buying and selling in the portfolio, and related matters than with the charges and fees.

125

The National Association for Variable Annuities (NAVA) does a study of company expenses for sales and marketing and for general expenses.[2] Companies use the study findings as benchmarks to indicate relative expense levels and indicate trends. However, NAVA does not suggest that the findings may be ranked for competitive purposes.

Similarly, while it is logical that companies with the most business on the books and/or selling the most would be able to spread their expenses over more units and thus be able to have products with the lowest charges and fees, this does not appear to be the case. One study[3] involving large variable annuity issuers showed the products to have both high and low charges and fees. Some of the newer products were higher than older products. The study concluded that there are no hard and fast rules about a variable annuity's cost and the size and experience of the company behind it. If comparisons are needed, it still is necessary to research the various products individually. The most reliable way of doing so is to read the respective prospectuses.

SECURITIES MARKETS IMPROVEMENT ACT

Prior to October 11, 1996, there was a regulatory "straight-jacket" which applied to the pricing of variable annuities. On that date, the National Securities Markets Improvement Act of 1996 was signed.[4] As discussed in Chapter 6, variable contracts are regulated as securities under the Securities Act of 1933 and as periodic payment plans under the Investment Company Act of 1940. Periodic payment plans are subject to heightened regulation that focuses on the types of sales loads and related charges allowed and the manner in which they may be deducted.[5] Consequently, variable contracts historically have been subject to regulation that goes far beyond that imposed on mutual funds or on most insurance and annuity products.

The National Securities Markets Improvement Act amended the Investment Company Act to require that aggregate fees and charges under a variable contract be "... reasonable in relation to the services rendered, the expenses expected to be incurred, and the risks assumed..." by the insurance company sponsoring the contract.[6]

There are two approaches to enforce the new reasonableness standard. First, an insurance company issuing a variable contract must affirmatively represent in the contract's registration statement that the fees and charges to be deducted meet the new reasonableness standard. Second, the SEC is authorized to make rules if variable contract charges become excessive.[7] The reasonableness representation does not have to be included in the product prospectus.

In determining whether the reasonableness standard applies, an insurer can take into account the nature and extent of services performed under the contract, the benefits conferred on the contract owner, and the nature and extent of the risks assumed by the insurer. Concerning sales loads, an insurer should consider the nature and quality of services necessary to ensure proper distribution of a particular contract. Thus, higher sales loads would be appropriate when relatively more selling effort is required. With respect to administrative charges, the nature and quality of the related administrative services should be considered.[8] All charges and fees must be considered in applying the reasonableness test, apparently including advisory fees charged to the various accounts.

Before the new law, there was no numerical limit on administrative charges but they were required to be "at cost." Now, administrative charges are one component of an aggregate charge which must be reasonable. The same is true of mortality and expense risk charges, a change from the SEC limit of 1.25%, plus additional charges for enhanced death benefits being assessed on a case-by-case basis. Sales loads are no longer subject to the 9% limitation of the Investment Company Act but to the aggregate charge which must be reasonable. However, National Association of Securities Dealers (NASD) Conduct Rule 2820 generally still limits variable annuity sales loads to 8.5% of premiums. The various fees may be combined and presented as one charge, although it appears the sales load must remain separate in order to demonstrate compliance with the NASD rule.[9]

No doubt, variable annuity issuers welcome the changes that have been made since the pricing atmosphere is more open and they can do more fashioning of the pricing to fit the products they are marketing and to fit their own operations. At the same time, the intense competition affecting these financial services products should keep charges and fees at levels in concert with reasonableness standards. It should not become necessary for the SEC to make new rules because charges have become excessive. However, the new law has just taken effect and not enough new products have been introduced or existing products changed to gauge the impact. What we may see is some significant changes in particular charges and fees that, in the aggregate, are reasonable and not much different from today. Yet, the changes might provide a competitive edge in the way the changed products perform under certain scenarios.

CONTRACT FEES

Some charges and fees are assessed to the contract as a whole and others are assessed to the various accounts. Many contracts have administration or contract fees, flat amounts, e.g., $30 or $40, to pay for maintenance of the contract, preparation of statements, premium notices, mailings, and other customer services. The flat fees are deducted pro rata from the various accounts in proportion to the assets in the accounts. They sometimes are described as "disappearing," since they are waived once the contract value or accumulation value of the variable annuity has reached a certain amount, e.g., $25,000 or $50,000. As mentioned below, a percentage of the assets, e.g., .25 percent, is subtracted to pay for similar expenses.

GUARANTEED ACCOUNT: INTEREST MARGIN

The charge assessed against the guaranteed or fixed account is indirect. It is an interest margin, the same system used with fixed annuities. The issuing company's investments in corporate bonds and government securities, for example, produce a certain rate of interest; then, a lesser rate is credited to the money in the guaranteed account. The difference between the two rates of interest, e.g., 2.25 percent (or 225 basis points), is the interest margin.

The size of the margin (or "haircut") depends on how large the expenses are that need to be covered, with the most immediate impact coming from sales expenses. Companies attempt to manage the margins so that the interest rates they guarantee do not need to fluctuate as frequently as the bond markets and so that the companies can hold some cash reserve against rising and falling market interest rates to remain competitive both with rates on new premiums and rates on renewing premiums.

Interest rate competitiveness is all the more important since the bonds and other securities being purchased often have maturity dates five or more years in the future and early liquidation, necessary to provide for customer cash withdrawals, will be at a discount. As a result, the company may find it difficult to pay the interest rate(s) it has promised. Surrender charges (discussed later in this chapter) also may help restrain customer withdrawals.

MORTALITY AND EXPENSE CHARGE

Definition

In addition to the administrative charge to assets, there is a mortality and expense (M & E) risk charge, a percentage subtracted from the variable accounts. M & E pays for three guarantees:

1. The guaranteed death benefit payable to the designated beneficiary;

2. The fixed payout options which guarantee that a certain amount will be paid for the life of the annuitant or annuitants; and

3. The guarantee that contract expenses will increase no more than the maximums stated in the prospectus.

The administrative expense charge and the M & E fee often are combined in a single charge, ranging from just over 1 percent to a little over 1.5 percent.

The mortality risk portion is affected by the type of guaranteed death benefit and by the payout amounts guaranteed in the contract. As discussed in Chapter 7, the higher the probable death benefit, due to enhanced or stepped-up provisions, the more is needed to pay for the benefit. Life income payout provisions are determined according to annuity tables which are used to estimate how long a person of a particular age and sex will live; guaranteed payout factors often are printed in the contract. When there are two or more annuitants, all lives must be considered. While the contract owner may elect instead to use annuity payout provisions currently in effect at the time income is to begin, the more favorable the provisions guaranteed in the contract are, the higher the mortality risk portion of the M & E fee needs to be.

When the M & E charge for one contract is higher than for another, there may be a variety of reasons. One reason may be that the issuing company has decided to make that fee higher and another fee in the contract lower. Another reason is that there may be more customer benefits being provided. For example, if the guaranteed death benefit is one which provides for generous enhancing or stepping up, there may be a need for a higher fee. Or if the contract provides for many other services, such as automatic rebalancing, internal dollar cost averaging, a large number of free transfers among accounts, etc., there may be such a need.

INVESTMENT MANAGEMENT FEES

Definition

Investment management fees are charged directly to each variable account and impact the performance figures of the account. They consist of both the investment advisory fee and a component covering other operating expenses. (Frequently, only the term investment advisory fee is used.) The operating expense portion is relatively small since services are being provided to only the insurance company variable account and not to a number of other shareholders. If expenses are such that it otherwise would be necessary to charge more than the maximum amount stated in the prospectus, typically a monthly percentage of assets in the account, the extra amount usually is absorbed and not charged to the account.

The investment advisory fee, also usually a monthly percentage of the assets in the account, is for the professional management of the investments in the account, a feature which many variable annuity buyers seek when they consider the advantages of variable annuities. The percentage amount of this fee depends on the type of account. The fee for accounts with only stocks or only corporate bonds and government securities might be lower than for accounts requiring more discretionary management such as balanced or asset allocation accounts which have a variety of types of investments and anticipate changes in the mix of investments on a regular basis. On the other hand, indexed accounts, which seek to emulate investments followed in external market indexes, such as the S & P 500, might have lower fees than the stock or bond accounts. International funds and special purpose accounts might have fees that are among the highest since they are apt to require specialized expertise and additional procedures.

The total investment management fee, which combines the advisory fee and some operating expense component, averages .77 percent, according to data of the National Association for Variable Annuities (NAVA).[10] Of course, an average cannot completely take into account the fact that different kinds of accounts require different kinds of investment management. Investment management fees are listed in the prospectus portions pertaining to the accounts but the fees themselves are not shown on the contract owner's summary of account activity. The account values shown on the account balance section will be net of the fees which have been charged and deducted from the accounts.

PROPRIETARY ACCOUNTS

When a variable annuity buyer allocates premiums to proprietary accounts, the variable accounts managed by investment advisors working for the company issuing the contract, the investment management fees are paid to the issuing company. When the buyer allocates to accounts managed by outside investment advisors, the outside advisors are paid the fees. Ordinarily, it is possible for the issuing company to provide the investment management and services at a lower cost because many of the services can be provided with systems and personnel already in place to serve other needs, or with relatively small incremental increases in systems and personnel. For that reason, the issuing company greatly prefers that buyers take advantage of their proprietary accounts.

On the other hand, outside managed accounts, especially those managed by organizations with well-known names, are very popular with the public and have been given credit for much of the increase in variable annuity sales. Issuing companies know this trend is good for them and seek out opportunities to include outside managed accounts not withstanding the fact that doing so may cause less to be allocated to their proprietary accounts. In the long run, the greater sales are expected to carry the day.

TRANSFER FEES

Transfers of values in one variable annuity account to other accounts may be made without the necessity of buying and selling and paying the resulting income taxes. As discussed in Chapter 7, there are some limitations but, generally, transfers are easily accomplished. While there are a variety of practices applicable to contracts, the current trend is for a certain number of transfers each year to be free of charge, with a fee, e.g., $10 or $20 applicable to additional transfers. The number of free transfers is enough to satisfy most variable annuity owner's needs, and additional transfers are charged only for a higher than usual number of transactions. The expense of free transfers is accounted for by the administrative charges and fees discussed above. Similarly, the expense of transfers, which are the result of internal dollar cost averaging and/or automatic rebalancing, are handled by those administrative charges and fees as well.

SURRENDER CHARGES

Example

Some of the most important charges associated with annuities, including variable annuities, are surrender charges. Surrender charges are applicable to surrenders or withdrawals from the contract value or accumulation value for a period of time. In nearly all products, surrender charges are applied when surrenders or withdrawals are made within a stated number of years following the payment of the premium. Typically, the charge is one which reduces each year following the premium payment until it has reduced to zero. For example, the charge may apply for eight years, but the percentage to be used reduces through the years:

Year	Percentage
1	7
2	7
3	6
4	5
5	4
6	3
7	2
8	1
9	0

In this example, if premiums are not paid for eight years, no surrender charges are made when the contract owner makes a surrender or withdrawal. Typically, there is a maximum surrender charge percentage, applicable to the contract as a whole. As discussed in Chapter 7, most contracts have surrender-charge-free withdrawals of

Caution

some sort. The most common provisions are those which provide that 10 percent, or sometimes 15 percent, of the contract value may be withdrawn in a contract year. Also, note that the surrender charge provisions applicable to withdrawals are apart from any tax penalties which may apply for premature distributions. Those provisions are discussed in Chapter 12.

Surrender charges are needed for several reasons. The most obvious one is the need for recovery of sales expenses when surrenders or large withdrawals occur early after the contract takes effect and/or premiums are paid. Few, if any, variable annuities have sales loads subtracted from premiums before they are paid into the various accounts. That is, essentially the full amount of premium is paid in. (A small, annual contract charge may be deducted, but such deductions frequently are made at the end of the year rather than at the beginning.) Sales expenses incurred, including sales representative and manager compensation, is recovered over a number of years as part of the interest margin on guaranteed accounts and by means of the contract fee and administrative fees charged to the contract.

If a contract owner surrenders or makes sizable withdrawals soon after making premium payments, there will be no time to recover the sales expenses. A surrender charge, assessed against surrenders or withdrawals, will help with the sales expenses recovery. The charge also serves the purpose of discouraging early surrenders and withdrawals for less than compelling reasons. The surrender-charge-free withdrawals that are available make it possible to obtain more limited amounts of cash on a regular basis.

A couple of other points should be made about surrender charges. As discussed in other contexts, the bonds and other securities, purchased by the issuing company to produce guaranteed rates of interest for premiums allocated to the guaranteed or fixed account, usually have maturities five or more years into the future. Early surrenders or withdrawals of account values will necessitate the selling of some of the securities held prior to maturity, usually at less than face value. Surrender charges will help compensate for the losses incurred as a result of the early sale of the securities. They also will discourage withdrawals and surrenders unless there has been a marked increase in market interest rates, an increase sufficient to overcome the effect of the surrender charges.

There are similar considerations with respect to the variable accounts. Most contract fees are asset-based, yet many of the expenses involved are less dependent on the amount of assets in the accounts. Most contract provisions and customer services must be provided without regard to the size of the accounts. Surrender charges will help recover some of the expenses incurred when asset-based charges and fees have been depressed because of early surrenders and withdrawals.

The assumption that is made when the various charges and fees are determined is that there will be a more-or-less consistent flow of premiums into and out of the contract. Surrender charges can serve to provide a reverse incentive for not interrupting this flow unnecessarily.

Some states impose a premium tax on variable annuity purchases. These taxes are payable by the purchaser and reduce contract or accumulation values, although they are collected at different times by different states. They range up to 4 percent but generally do not exceed 2 percent.

GROUP ANNUITY PRICING

Planning Tips

To this point, the discussion of pricing has been concerned primarily with individual variable annuities. Group annuities, which usually include separate variable accounts, are used to fund qualified retirement plans in particular. The great popularity of 401(k) plans in recent years has extended the use of group annuities to smaller and smaller plans. A rule of thumb is that plans involving fifteen or more participants probably will be better served with group annuities than with a collection of individual variable annuities. Group annuities, used in many qualified retirement plans, are not registered products because they are being marketed to plans, not to individual participants. The requirements of these plans include many of the same disclosure and procedural safeguards as registered products.

Group annuity pricing includes the same sorts of asset-based fees. There also are contract charges and participant level charges. There is more latitude with respect to the handling of sales expense loads than with individual variable annuities. Some of these group cases are very large and fees and charges become very competitive. Existing cases which are taken over from another issuer might have different loads, charges and fees applicable to existing assets and/or existing participants than those applicable to new participants and/or additions to existing accounts. In some cases, the sales compensation agreed to may consist only of asset-based fees with no compensation otherwise for new premiums produced. In other cases, combinations of sales commissions and asset-based compensation may be used. Thus, the pricing of group annuities and of individual variable annuities is somewhat different, although composed of many of the same factors and considerations.

OPERATIONAL DIFFERENCES

There are some operational differences between group annuities and individual variable annuities. The group annuity customer is the employer or other plan sponsor; the individuals are plan participants who have their business relationship with the plan sponsor, rather than the issuing company. Although many customer services are provided by the issuing company to plan participants, they are being provided in the name of the plan sponsor.

Such items as changes of investments and reallocations are made by participant request to the plan sponsor. There may be limitations on the timing and frequency of such changes. Withdrawals may be more limited with respect to timing and frequency. With individual variable annuities, the annuity buyer is the customer and the business relationship is between the customer and the issuing company directly. We already have referred to the owner's right to make changes virtually at will, the fact that his/her investment and other options are many, and that there is a great variety of withdrawal and payout provisions.

On the other hand, a group annuity and an individual variable annuity, from the individual's point of view, may look quite similar. The same sorts of premium allocations often are available, as are the same sorts of variable account choices and the same methods of paying premiums into the accounts. However, when the group annuities are used inside qualified retirement plans, there are differences having to do with taxation of premiums (plan contributions) and with some payout options, among others. Qualified retirement plans are discussed in Chapter 11.

COMPARISONS AND CUSTOMER VALUE

This chapter began with the need to design a product that is a good customer value as well as one that will be profitable for the issuing company. As discussed in Chapter 5, good customer value also includes satisfaction with having taken concrete steps to save and invest, rather than remaining on the sideline, and satisfaction with the way the product purchases were made. Additionally, good customer value encompasses a good experience with the sales representative: good advice and helpfulness, someone who listens, a good person to do business with; an expectation of a quality issuing company: good, efficient procedures, helpful and complete sales literature, the likelihood that future communications and transactions will flow smoothly; and quality product performance as a result of good investment management. The product is very important but all of these factors go into the complete package that is embodied in the relationship among the customer, sales representative and company.

Purchasing registered products is done in an atmosphere of relatively high disclosure. There is considerably more easily obtained information available about the charges, fees, and operation of variable annuity contracts than about most things we purchase. Not infrequently, such detailed information about many consumer products can be had but only by going to considerable effort involving extra time. With registered products, most of it is right there in the prospectus, albeit sometimes requiring effort to "wade through" the language. Some people are detail oriented and enjoy making their own discoveries by reading the prospectus and sales literature. Others are put off by the detail and depend on sales representatives to point out pertinent information to them. But at least, the information is at hand and can be referred to in concrete terms.

Reminder

When comparing one financial services product with another, it is important to remember the relationship between those features that the potential customer believes are needed and the stated charges and fees which relate to them. Put another way, a small difference in a charge or fee between one product and another is important only to the extent that the charge or fee is important to the potential customer. For example, we see in Chapter 7 the variety of death benefits, withdrawal arrangements, transfers and transfer fees, and other product features; differences usually result in some variations in charges and fees. But how important are they to the customer? How "big a deal" should be made of the differences? Is this "much ado about nothing"? One of the most consistently made comparisons is between variable annuities and mutual funds. The issues involved in those comparisons are similar, and are taken up in more detail in Chapter 10.

CHAPTER FOOTNOTES

1. Ruark, Timothy J., FSA, MAAA, "Variable Annuities: Managing the Risks," *NAVA Outlook*, November/December, 1995.

2. Koco, Linda, "NAVA's '95 Expense Study Creates VA Benchmarks," *National Underwriter*, Life and Health/Financial Services edition, October 7, 1996.

3. Strickland, Jennifer, "Large VA Insurers Don't Always Have Lowest Fees," *National Underwriter*, Life and Health/Financial Services edition, March 24, 1997.

4. National Securities Markets Improvement Act of 1996, P.L. 104-290.

5. Conner, W. Thomas and Mackey, Mark J., "Variable Contract Charges Simplified," *NAVA Outlook*, November, Special Edition, 1996. Blazzard, Norse N. and Hasenauer, Judith A., "Law May Change Structure of Variable Products," *National Underwriter*, Life and Health/Financial Services edition, November 11, 1996.

6. National Securities Markets Improvement Act of 1996, P.L. 104-290, Section 205 (e) (2) (A).

7. Conner, W. Thomas and Mackey, Mark J., "Variable Contract Charges Simplified," *NAVA Outlook*, November, Special Edition, 1996. Blazzard, Norse N. and Hasenauer, Judith A., "Law May Change Structure of Variable Products," *National Underwriter*, Life and Health/Financial Services edition, November 11, 1996.

8.   *Ibid.*

9.   *Ibid*; NASD Conduct Rules, Rule 2820, "Variable Contracts of an Insurance Company - (c) Sales Charges." *National Association of Securities Dealers Manual.*

10. *Variable Annuities: An Attractive Choice for a More Secure Retirement,* National Association for Variable Annuities, 1996.

9

DISTRIBUTION OF PRODUCTS

VARIETY OF DISTRIBUTION OUTLETS

Variable annuity products are developed by insurance companies alone or by insurance companies in conjunction or joint venture with other organizations such as mutual fund companies. The insurance companies' know-how in product development, dealing with life contingencies, annuitization, and death benefits and the investment management personnel they already have in place are put to use as products are developed. Additional investment management and development costs can be supplied by the joint venture partners. On the other hand, variable annuities are distributed by a large number of different organizations and there appears to be significant change on the horizon.

According to the Variable Annuity Research & Data Service (VARDS) year end report for 1996,[1] 43 percent of the sales in the survey in 1996 were sold by agents directly associated with insurance companies, 19 percent were sold by regional investment firms, 12 percent by independent NASD firms, 11 percent by New York brokerage firms, 11 percent by banks and credit unions, and 4 percent by direct response selling. The VARDS editors expect that by the end of the year 2000, the bank and credit union share will have grown from 11 percent to 20 percent, New York brokerage firms to 16 percent, independent NASD firms to 14 percent, and direct response sales to 7 percent. The sources expected to lose share are agents directly associated with insurance companies, from 43 percent to 30 percent, and regional investment firms, from 19 percent to 13 percent.

As financial services reform legislation is adopted which makes it possible for banks and other financial institutions to take on more and more of the functions that only insurance companies are able to do at present, it stands to reason that these other institutions will increase their share of variable annuity sales. They will be able to profit from the manufacturing of products as well as the distribution of them. Even before these changes, insurance companies are constantly looking for sales distribution outlets and many of them are turning more and more to banks as well as to the other sources expected to increase distribution share.

PRODUCER COMPENSATION

Annuity producers are compensated in at least two ways, though both methods are not used with all products. The first is a percentage of the premium paid by the annuity buyer. The second is a percentage of the assets being managed in the various accounts, sometimes referred to as "trailer commissions." There is a relatively wide range of compensation patterns although, in the end, variable annuity sales loads are limited by NASD Rule 2820 to 8.5 percent of premiums.[2]

The wide range comes about because of the variety of products, especially involving minimum initial and continuing premiums, any specialized markets where the products are to be used, and how the products are being distributed. For example, products with high initial premiums sometimes are marketed for special uses. Perhaps, they are being marketed exclusively to a particular group of buyers. In these instances, the compensation on premiums may be on the low side, with asset-based compensation somewhat higher than usual. Products used primarily for rollovers from qualified plans or as substitutes in existing plans may rely almost exclusively on asset-based compensation.

Products distributed by agents and other registered representatives who are responsible for developing their own customers usually pay more compensation based more on premiums and less on assets. How high these commissions are depends, in part, on the level of services being provided by the broker/dealer and insurance company. Generally, if relatively few services are provided the compensation is higher than when a greater number of services is provided. The services we are referring to here include sales consultation, sales training and compliance assistance, breadth of product line, access to certain fringe benefits, applicability of sales credits to sales conference qualification, and the like. Compensation of both types also is paid to local office or agency management.

When products are distributed through sources where the individual producers do not have to develop individual customers, such as banks or credit unions, producer compensation usually is lower. Of course, the total compensation paid to the bank or credit union also includes amounts for developing customers and administrative costs.

PAID TO OTHER DISTRIBUTORS

Compensation otherwise paid to agents or sales representatives and to managers is paid to the bank, credit union, or other financial institution; it is up to that institution to decide how much of this amount is paid to the individual producers. This is similar to the arrangement a broker/dealer makes to distribute a group of mutual funds. The mutual fund group pays what is called a "dealer concession" to the broker/

dealer which then decides how much of it must be retained for expenses and how much is to be paid to producers and agency or local office management personnel. The arrangement the broker/dealer makes with producers often varies according to the producers' level of production.

It is likely that an insurance company will pay more in these situations than it would have paid to agents and managers. That is because the financial institution will perform many of the services and undergo many of the costs that the insurance company or broker/dealer otherwise would have been responsible for assuming. It is not unusual for an insurance company and broker/dealer to determine that although they are paying more in compensation for business produced by other financial institutions, the total direct and indirect costs of producing the business are lower than for business produced by agents with whom they have a direct relationship. However, the associated question of whether or not that business will enjoy as favorable premium persistency as business produced by associated agents needs to be taken into consideration. A continuing flow of premiums into contracts helps attain the critical mass needed in accounts to make them profitable. The number of withdrawals from accounts also may be different for customers of the various distribution sources.

PERCENTAGES PAID

The percentage of premiums paid to producers can range from zero, as indicated above, to 3½, or 4 percent, to 5 percent and higher. The percentage of premiums paid to managers usually is lower, ranging from less than 1 percent to 2 percent or more. In the past, compensation arrangements sometimes had somewhat higher percentages paid during the first year or several years and lower percentages paid thereafter. Most of today's arrangements use constant percentages on all premiums intended to be continuing. Single premium products often have different percentages from their continuing premium counterparts. Sometimes, percentages vary by size of the premium being paid.

The percentage of assets or trailer commission rate also varies although not over so great a range. Most asset percentages are less than 1 percent, perhaps ⅛, ¼, or ½ of 1 percent. Of course, over time, this fraction of a percent is applied to a larger and larger number until the compensation involved is substantial indeed. In some cases, there is a floor level of assets which must be reached before the percentage of assets compensation is paid. This is so that elaborate administrative systems do not have to be implemented for producers who only occasionally produce business.

Compensation arrangements which have both a percentage of premiums and a percentage of assets usually make use of a see-saw principle. The higher the asset percentage, the lower the premium percentage, and vice versa. As we have seen in Chapter 8, there is only so much that can be paid for the production of business, whether it is because of the need for the product to be profitable and competitive, or because of limitations imposed by NASD or SEC rules.

It is not unusual for the compensation on fixed annuities to be higher, especially with respect to the percentage of premiums, than on variable annuities. Fixed annuities are not subject to NASD or SEC rules. But more than that, some fixed annuities are designed with features that allow for higher sales costs to be built into the price. For example, some interest rates declared are conditioned on the annuity being annuitized later. If the annuity holder surrenders instead of annuitizing, a deduction is made from contract values, thus providing a source to make up for the additional compensation that has been paid. Other features relate to the length of interest rate guarantees and the like. For the most part, it is not possible to design variable annuities with these sorts of features.

INCREASING COMPENSATION

As seems clear, a producer of variable annuities earns more compensation by selling more premiums, by keeping premiums continuing on contracts sold earlier, and where applicable, by constantly building his/her book of business so that the percentage of assets compensation is applied to an ever increasing figure.

Selling more premiums each year than the year before obviously increases percentage of premium commissions from new sales. Not quite so obvious is the beneficial effect of customers continuing to pay premiums as planned and of assets continuing to grow so that percentage of assets commissions increase.

Planning Tips

Registered representatives usually put most of their effort into finding, approaching and selling new customers. As we see here, considerable effort also needs to be directed at keeping in consistent contact with existing customers so that they will remain happy enough to continue paying the premiums they have planned to pay. Consistent contact with customers also will uncover any disappointments serious enough to motivate customers to withdraw funds from their contracts and put them elsewhere.

MAKING A PROFIT

To conclude this discussion, we should look at how the insurance company, and joint venture partner, make money from developing and marketing variable annuities. Simply stated, it is from having income exceed expenses. As discussed in Chapter 8, sources of income are contract fees, interest margins, mortality and expense charges, transfer fees, surrender charges, and on accounts being managed, investment management fees. Investment management fees vary according to the types of accounts involved. Not all of these charges and fees will be received on every contract. For example, if little or no money is in the guaranteed account, there will be little or no interest margin. If few transfers are made, few transfer fees, if any, will be charged. If there are no early surrenders, there will be no surrender charges levied. The pricing actuary must use realistic assumptions as to how much revenue can be obtained from the various sources in the aggregate. When actuaries set charges and fees, they must consider competition. In order to be competitive, the charges and fees must be set at levels without much "wiggle" room.

Definition

We also have discussed the need for critical mass — enough assets in the various accounts to spread the costs of managing and administering the accounts so that the cost can be covered by the investment management fee being charged to each contract. In this context, the persistency of premiums coming into the accounts and the assets remaining there for a period of time are important. In earlier discussions, we mentioned the fact that companies prefer that their proprietary accounts be used extensively because some of the administrative costs are being absorbed elsewhere in the company and the investment management fees being charged can go further. In other words, proprietary accounts usually are more profitable.

Distribution expenses must be kept in line if the products are to be profitable. Often, the best thing that can happen is for there to be more sales so that critical mass is achieved earlier in the product's life. For this to happen, there often is a need to acquire more distribution sources. This means more production from registered representatives from the ranks of existing offices and sources as well as increasing the number of representatives in those offices. It also means contracting with sources not previously used for distribution, a tactic that must be carried out carefully. Not infrequently, disappointment arises due to misunderstandings and a mismatch between the new producers contracted and the existing products available for sale.

While increased production will help, controlling expenses also is essential. Reaching potential new customers has become more and more difficult, and sometimes more costly. Additional time and money is needed to find new customers. People's service expectations can be met only through the use of more and more technology. While the costs of hardware and off-the-shelf software constantly are falling, the costs of needed proprietary software have not. Local offices are faced with cost increases for office space, services and administrative personnel. Yet, in a competitive atmosphere that is apt only to intensify, commission compensation can increase only by selling more, keeping premiums coming in on contracts in force and building the overall book of business.

At the same time, expense increases must be kept within reasonable limits. When all is said and done, these are the factors faced by nearly all business people today.

CHAPTER FOOTNOTES

1. "Special Report, Year-End (12/31/96) Sales and Asset Survey", *The Variable Annuity and Research Data Service (VARDS)*, Financial Planning Resources, Inc.

2. NASD Conduct Rules, Rule 2820, "Variable Contracts of an Insurance Company - (c) Sales Charges." *National Association of Securities Dealers Manual.*

10

OTHER FINANCIAL SERVICES PRODUCTS

As we have seen throughout this book, variable annuities are excellent financial services product choices for a great number of people. However, even the most ardent variable annuity advocate would not insist that they are the only choice. Rather, they should play a prominent role in many people's overall financial plans which should also include other products. In this chapter, we consider some of the more prominent other products and, to an extent where appropriate, compare and contrast them with variable annuities. This chapter is intended to touch many of the high points but not to be an exhaustive discussion.

STOCKS AND BONDS

Definition

Stocks and bonds traded on national and regional exchanges receive the most publicity in the general press. A share of stock represents ownership of a corporation and constitutes a claim on the corporation's earnings and assets. Common stock usually entitles the shareholder to vote in the election of directors and other matters taken up at shareholders meetings or by proxy. Preferred stock generally does not confer voting rights but it has prior claim on assets and earnings. That is, dividends must be paid on preferred stock before any can be paid on common stock. A corporation can authorize additional classes of stock, each with its own set of contractual rights.

Common stock prices are the ones most often quoted in news accounts of the stock market, and the ones that usually rise and fall most substantially. When people talk about stocks keeping pace with inflation, it is common stocks they are describing. On the other hand, many investors like to hedge against some risk by investing a portion of their money in preferred stock. Though the preferred stock probably will not appreciate as much as the common, it will stand ahead of the common shares in the dividend paying line.

Definition

A bond is an interest-bearing or discounted government or corporate security that obligates the issuer to pay the bondholder a specified return, usually at specific intervals, and to repay the principal amount of the loan at maturity. Bondholders are creditors of the government agency or corporation, but they have no corporate ownership privileges. A secured bond is one backed by specific collateral, which the bondholder may sell if the issuer fails to pay interest or principal when due. More common are unsecured bonds, referred to as debentures, which are backed by the full faith and credit of the issuer but not by any specific collateral. A convertible bond is one that the bondholder may exchange for some other securities, usually stock of the issuing company, at some future date under certain conditions. A callable bond is one that may be redeemed by the issuer before the scheduled maturity. The issuer must pay the holders a premium price if the bond is retired early. Bonds usually are called when interest rates fall so significantly that the issuer can save money by floating new bonds at lower rates.

Most stocks and bonds are traded on national securities exchanges, such as the New York Stock Exchange or the American Stock Exchange, or over the counter where they are tracked, in large part, on the NASDAQ (National Association of Securities Dealers Automated Quotation system). NASDAQ is a computerized system that provides brokers and dealers with price quotations for over the counter as well as many New York Stock Exchange listed securities. NASDAQ quotes are published on the financial pages of most newspapers. Stocks and bonds also are listed on regional exchanges; some are available for sale only in particular states.

Definition

People may purchase treasury securities directly or through a broker or registered representative, although they also are purchased for certain mutual funds and variable accounts of variable annuities. Treasury securities are negotiable obligations of the U.S. government, secured by its full faith and credit, and issued at various schedules with various maturities. The income from treasury securities is exempt from state and local income taxes but not from federal taxes. Treasury bills have maturities of one-year or less and are issued at a discount from the face value. Treasury notes are intermediate securities with maturities of from one to ten years. Denominations range from $1,000 to $1 million or more. Treasury bonds are long-term instruments with maturities of 10 years or longer and are issued in minimum denominations of $1,000.

We have referred many times to the usual methods of purchasing variable annuities; they are purchased through a registered representative who is associated with a broker/dealer which has an agreement to market one or more products of an insurance company. The insurance company sends regular premium notices which give the purchaser the opportunity to make additional purchases. The purchaser also has the right to make a number of adjustments in the variable accounts, thereby performing the functions of buying and selling among the accounts. We also have referred to the diversification and the professional investment management available when variable annuities are purchased.

Most of what has just been mentioned is different when the investor buys stocks and bonds directly. (Remember that the variable annuity purchaser buys shares of the variable accounts, not shares of the stocks and bonds bought for the variable accounts.) An investor may buy stocks and bonds in a number of ways, the most common being through a stock broker after consultation, and perhaps a recommendation, by that broker. Today, there is great variety in the level of services being provided by various brokerage firms, from what is called complete service, including consultation, research, recommendations, and the like, to a number of different kinds of discount brokerage services. As should be expected, the size of the sales charges has much to do with the level of services. People who want to do their own investigating and decision making often opt for a low level of service with a commensurate level of sales charge. Much of their work, including the purchases themselves, can be done over the telephone or on the internet.

Selecting Investments

People who feel competent to do so may enjoy selecting their own investments, whether they do so largely independently or after consultation with a broker. For example, when they select the stock of a company that does better than similar companies in the same industry or better than others they might have selected, they are rewarded, monetarily and psychologically.

But as we have seen earlier, many people do not feel competent to make their own selections. Even more people do not feel competent nor have the time to continue making stock and bond selections on an ongoing basis. That is the reason for "hiring" professional investment managers through a variable annuity.

Stock brokers can help individual investors on a continuing basis but they are not really being paid to be professional investment managers in the usual sense. Investors with relatively large holdings often retain professional investment advisors to look after their accounts for a fee. Stock brokers can serve the purpose of encouraging the investor to continue making new purchases, investing more money in order to achieve the investor's future goals. This may or may not be as effective as regular premium notices and other contacts by the variable annuity issuer and registered representative.

Caution

The person who selects his/her own stocks and bonds needs to have a reasonable level of diversification in order to spread risk. Obviously, it is easier to attain proper diversification when the investor has the funds to purchase a substantial number of stocks and bonds. It is not so easy for the person starting out or the person who has limited funds available for investing. And in order to achieve proper diversification, an investor must select the right stocks and bonds, even more investment selection. Diversification is easier to achieve by purchasing shares of variable annuity accounts which already are diversified; and that is even more the case when the investor has limited funds to invest. Another option for investors in this situation is the purchase of mutual fund shares, as discussed below.

Income Tax

The income tax aspects connected with buying individual stocks and bonds also are different from those applicable to variable annuities. Generally, earnings and gains from stocks and bonds are taxed currently; there is no deferral of earnings as is the case with variable annuities. On the other hand, capital gains arising when stocks are sold are taxed at rates which are generally lower than ordinary income rates. No capital gains treatment is available with variable annuities.

Since there is no deferral of income with stocks and bonds, there is no concern with penalties arising when premature distributions are made, as is the case with variable annuities. An important exception to the current taxation of earnings and interest is municipal bonds, debt obligations of state or local governmental entities. The interest from many of these is exempt from federal income tax and some also are exempt from state income tax. The interest income is completely exempt, not merely deferred to another time. (There is a limit on how much tax-exempt income a taxpayer can receive without triggering an additional tax, the alternative minimum tax.)

DERIVATIVE INVESTMENTS

Definition

Before leaving the subject of stock marketing investing, we should mention derivative investments which include options and futures. Options are rights to buy or sell property that are granted in exchange for agreed-upon sums. If a right is not exercised after a specified period, the option expires and the option buyer forfeits the sum paid. Options are associated with transactions tied to stocks, commodities, and stock indexes. They are traded on many exchanges. A call option gives its buyer the right to buy shares (usually 100 shares) of the underlying security at a fixed price before a specified date in the future, usually three, six or nine months. A put option gives its buyer the right to sell a specified number of shares of a stock at a particular price within a specified period of time. The call option buyer speculates that the price of the stock will rise during the period and he/she will be able to buy at a bargain. The put option buyer speculates in the opposite direction-that the price will fall and he/she will be able to sell at the option price instead.

Definition

A futures contract is an agreement to buy or sell a specific amount of a commodity or a financial instrument at a particular price on a stipulated future date. The price is established between buyer and seller on the floor of a commodity exchange, using what is referred to as the open outcry system. A futures contract obligates the buyer to purchase the underlying commodity and the seller to sell it, unless the contract is sold to another before the settlement date. The obligation passes to the buyer of the contract. This contrasts with options where the person chooses whether or not to exercise the option by the exercise date.

MUTUAL FUNDS

The financial services product that is most similar to a variable annuity is a mutual fund. In fact, variable annuities often are described as mutual funds with a tax shelter, referring to the deferral of current income tax on the interest and earnings in the variable annuity accounts while the funds remain inside the contract.

Describing the two products with respect to each other in this way is an oversimplification. There are some significant differences. More than that, the two are often competitors for the same investors' savings and investments. In part, this is because of the great number of similarities. Both variable annuities and mutual funds can be purchased in convenient amounts on a regular basis. There is professional investment management and diversification. The variable accounts in variable annuities are managed by people who also manage mutual funds. There is a ready market for the sale of shares; they will be repurchased by the fund when the investor wants them redeemed.

Numerous articles attempt to point out how mutual funds are better for certain people than variable annuities. The usual arguments point out the greater variety of mutual funds and assert that mutual funds have lower charges because they do not have the mortality and expense (M & E) charges that variable annuities do. There is no question that there are more mutual funds available to buy than variable annuities, although there is a question as to just how many choices are enough to suit the needs of the overwhelming majority of persons who would like to save and invest in this way. The product charges are another matter. The question there is whether the additional charges in the variable annuity are worth paying, given the additional provisions and features available.

At times, the competition between mutual funds and variable annuities seems a bit strange. Most registered representatives who market variable annuities also market mutual funds. They are in a position to provide whichever product is the right one for the customer. What sometimes happens is that one registered representative recommends a mutual fund and a different one recommends a variable annuity, even though both representatives could have provided either. In such a case, arguments should center on which product is better for the customer rather than which product seems to be better when compared with the other standing apart from the customer.

Planning Tips

There is another aspect to this. While a registered representative may be able to provide both products, the organization preparing the sales arguments may not be so situated. It must prepare materials designed to sell its products without regard for any knowledge of a particular customer. The fact is, many people feel that head-on comparisons between mutual funds and variable annuities should be avoided. If made forcefully enough, the comparisons may confuse customers enough for them to avoid or put off buying either. However, there are differences which we should look at.

Both mutual funds and variable annuities have investment expense charges. The charges for mutual funds tend to be higher than those for variable annuities. But variable annuities also have M & E charges which, when added to the investment expense charges, total more than the mutual fund investment expense charges.[1] One reason the investment expense charges can be less for variable annuities is that some of the administration charges are handled by the insurance company which issues the variable annuity. Presumably, the associated costs are handled through a portion of the M & E charge.

VARIABLE ANNUITY FEATURES

Planning Tips

As mentioned above, variable annuities have features and provisions which mutual funds do not have. The first is the deferral of recognition of current income due to interest and earnings while funds remain inside the contract and are not withdrawn. Only mutual funds inside IRAs and other plans have this type of deferral. It should be pointed out here that some of the annual mutual fund income to be reported is capital gains, which is generally taxed more favorably than at ordinary income rates. Variable annuity earnings do not produce capital gains. Obviously, since mutual funds have no income deferral, no penalty taxes apply to premature distributions.

A related provision is the fact that money inside a variable annuity can be transferred from one account to another without any sales or new purchases resulting in recognition of gains (or losses). With mutual funds, changes can be made within mutual fund families with a minimum of expense but there is recognition of gain (or loss) when one fund is sold and another purchased, even within the same family of funds. Annuities also may be exchanged for each other on a tax-free basis under Code Section 1035, as discussed further in Chapter 12. Following such an exchange, the deferral of recognition of income on interest and earnings continues with the new annuity contract.

**Planning
Tips**

Variable annuities have death benefits which can amount to considerably more than the value of a mutual fund which will pass to a family member when the mutual fund owner dies. Additionally, variable annuities offer fixed and variable life income options. This means a person can receive an income for his/her life, no matter how long. It also means that since principal and earnings are combined in the income payment, it is possible for a person at retirement age to receive more income than would be the case if only interest and earnings from a mutual fund or other financial product were the source of income. For those of more modest means, this is a very important feature. With mutual funds, a person may withdraw both principal and earnings, but there is no guarantee that the money will last for the person's lifetime.

There is a point of comparison related to the performance of mutual funds and variable annuities. When one of the customer's primary objectives is to provide for retirement, it may be that variable annuities are a better choice due to product performance. This is due to the fact that the investment manager can consider a longer horizon for selecting investments. The buyer will not be looking for such immediate results as would be the case if the horizon were shorter. Also, the manager needs less invested in liquid assets which can be redeemed quickly. The tax deferral, possible penalties, and surrender charges in the early years of the variable annuity strongly discourage taking withdrawals from the contract.

Earlier in this part of the discussion, we stated that many people argue that variable annuity-mutual fund comparisons should be avoided. Though we have pointed out some of the differences here, the argument to avoid comparisons is a good one. The comparisons which are published use averages whether they pertain to expense charges, performance or other criteria. Though data on the particular products a customer is considering are available from prospectuses and other published materials, how the products work in actual usage can only be determined retrospectively. A customer probably has enough to think about when he/she considers goals and objectives, the selection of fixed and variable accounts, and how much money to put in each one, without considering additionally the inside charges and fees, unless those charges and fees are out of line with other, similar products. As indicated previously, nothing good comes if the customer does not put anything into any decent product.

Reminder

WRAP ACCOUNTS

We should mention mutual fund wrap accounts here, which are more a service than a financial services product, although they do produce revenue. Wrap accounts charge a fee for analyzing a customer's investment needs, developing an appropriate asset allocation strategy, and selecting a portfolio of mutual funds. The basic services include a point of sale program, which is either paper-based or software-based, that assesses investors' risk profiles, investment objectives, time horizon , and suitability. The fee is based in part on percentages of assets and in part on certain flat charges. Generally, a relatively large amount of assets is needed for the fee to be justified and, as a result, wrap accounts frequently have minimum asset requirements for participation.

LIMITED PARTNERSHIPS AND UNIT INVESTMENT TRUSTS

Limited partnerships have at least one general partner in addition to the many limited partners. General partners manage a project and limited partners invest in it. (Limited here refers to the fact that the limited partner's financial liability in the enterprise is limited to what he/she has invested. Creditors cannot go beyond the investment to the partner's personal assets, as is the case with general partners.) Typically, limited partnerships invest in real estate, oil and gas, and equipment leasing, but they may also finance movies, research and development and other projects. Public limited partnerships usually are sold through brokerage firms and broker/dealers.[2] Also, there are private limited partnerships which usually call for far fewer limited partners who invest larger amounts.

Definition

A unit investment trust purchases a fixed portfolio of income-producing securities, such as corporate, municipal, or government bonds, mortgage-backed securities, or preferred stock. Units in the trust are sold by brokers to investors for a load charge (e.g., 4 percent). Unit holders receive an undivided interest in both the principal and the income portion of the portfolio in proportion to the amount of money they invest. The portfolio remains fixed until all the securities mature and unit holders have recovered their principal. Most brokerage firms maintain a secondary market in the trusts they sell, so that units can be resold if necessary.[3]

Limited partnerships and unit investment trusts are invested in by a number of people, especially when they suit an investor's needs better than more common investments such as stocks, bonds, mutual funds, and variable annuities. In the recent past, some income tax provisions pertaining to limited partnerships made them particularly attractive. Eventually, Congress decided the provisions were too favorable and changed them. As a result, choosing to invest in limited partnerships is influenced more by their investment potential in accomplishing the investor's goals than by their income tax aspects.

REAL ESTATE

Nearly all people invest in real estate; they do so when they buy their homes. One of the usual considerations is how easily and for what price a home may be sold later. There always is the hope that the real estate will increase in value so that it can be sold for more than was paid and the proceeds used to purchase a more expensive home. As a result, nearly everyone knows something about investing in real estate. People know that there are up markets and down markets. They have seen people "make a killing" in an up market by selling for far more than comparable homes in the recent past. They also have seen people not be able to sell their homes in a down market, and later "take a beating" by having to sell at considerably less than they paid not long ago.

Beyond buying homes, a number of people invest in other real estate by buying homes or buildings that are for sale. Sometimes, the people plan to rent the property and make a gain from rental income over the mortgage payments and maintenance expenses. Sometimes, they plan to improve the property and sell it for a higher price, usually within a relatively short period of time. With either of these approaches, those who know how to do maintenance and make improvements at a reasonable cost usually are better off.

Caution

People generally are pretty realistic about real estate investing because they have first-hand experience. There was a time when the prevailing view was that all real estate appreciates. Today, there is a more balanced view. Sometimes you win and sometimes you do not, but timing is extremely important and the investor must be in a position to "ride out" any temporary depression in the market. And to be successful at real estate investing, you have to know what you are doing. Rarely are there reports and studies available to review. And while there is much more disclosure required today on real estate sales contracts, there still is ample opportunity to miss important factors and make costly mistakes. As indicated, there is no ready market when the investor wants to sell, such as with variable annuity variable accounts, mutual funds, and the stock exchanges and over-the-counter market. Real estate cannot be purchased in convenient quantities which may be changed frequently. There is no SEC or NASD to require adequate disclosure. Still, for those who are adept, there are good opportunities in real estate investing.

Definition

There are at least two ways of investing in real estate without actually purchasing particular pieces of property. One is through limited partnerships, as mentioned above. The other is through Real Estate Investment Trusts (REITs). REITs, usually traded publicly, manage a portfolio of real estate to earn profits for shareholders. They make diverse investments in real estate from shopping centers and office buildings to apartment complexes and hotels. Equity REITs take equity positions in real estate; shareholders receive income from the rents received from the properties and receive capital gains as buildings are sold at a profit. Mortgage REITs specialize in lending money to building developers; they pass interest income on to shareholders. Some REITs have a mixture of equity and debt investments. In order to avoid a corporate income tax, REITs must receive 75 percent or more of their income from real estate and 95 percent of their taxable income must be distributed to shareholders.[4]

SAVINGS ACCOUNTS AND CERTIFICATES OF DEPOSIT

Of course, one of the most frequently used methods of accumulating savings is through savings accounts and certificates of deposit. Savings accounts are highly liquid in that withdrawals may be made from them at any time, an important point in some situations. The chief disadvantage to savings accounts is that their interest rates are low. That is because of the need for such a high degree of liquidity.

Certificates of deposit, generally referred to as CDs, pay higher rates of interest but they are purchased for a certain period of time (e.g., 3 months, 6 months, 24 months, 36 months, etc). Generally, the longer the period the higher the rate, although sometimes there is not much difference. If there is a need to redeem the certificates before the period has run, a penalty applies, thereby having the effect of reducing the interest rate paid. Most people have at least some of their savings in savings accounts, CDs or interest-bearing checking accounts.

IN CONCLUSION

As we have seen, there are a great many outlets for people's savings and investment dollars. Some require more knowledge, care and attention than others. Some are easier to learn about than others because of the amount of information that is published and otherwise made available to the public. Some provide the opportunity to invest in equities, in order to attempt to keep pace with inflation, and some do not. Some have guaranteed minimum interest rates and some do not. Some are easier to purchase in convenient amounts and at convenient times than others. Some have tax advantages over others at certain times. Some are easier to take income from, whether on a regular basis or from time to time, than others. Some are better than others at maximizing income at retirement time. Some are easier to redeem or resell than others when the time comes for that action. And most importantly, some will have more attributes needed and desired by a particular customer than others.

CHAPTER FOOTNOTES

1. Rohda, Rodney R., "The Real Cost of a Variable Annuity 1995 Update," *NAVA Outlook*, May/June, 1995; Murphy, Richard C. "The Real Cost of a Variable Annuity-1996 Update," *NAVA Outlook*, March/April, 1996.

2. *Dictionary of Finance and Investment Terms*, Barron's Educational Series, Inc.

3. *Ibid.*

4. *Ibid.*

11

VARIABLE ANNUITIES IN BUSI-
NESS AND ESTATE PLANNING

QUALIFIED RETIREMENT PLANS

As mentioned in earlier chapters, variable annuities have uses in business, particularly in retirement plans, and to some extent in estate planning. The discussions in this chapter are intended to be of an overview nature so that the places where variable annuities may be used can be identified. Treating the subjects fully requires much more development and is beyond the scope of this book. We begin with qualified retirement plans.

Qualified retirement plans, which include pension, annuity, profit sharing and stock bonus plans, are particularly attractive because of their tax advantages:

1. The employer can take a current business expense deduction for its contributions to the plan even though the employees are not currently taxed on the them[1];

2. Generally, an employee pays no tax until the benefits are distributed[2];

3. A lump sum distribution meeting certain requirements may be eligible for special tax treatment[3];

4. Annuity and installment payments are taxable only as received[4]; and

5. The fund within the plan earns and compounds income on a tax free basis.[5]

Definition

A pension is defined as a plan established and maintained by an employer primarily to provide systematically for the payment of definitely determinable benefits to employees over a period of years, usually for life, after retirement. Definitely determinable benefits are provided by having either fixed benefits (also called defined benefits) or fixed contributions. Under a defined benefit plan, the size of the pension, or a formula to determine size, is set in advance, and by actuarial methods the annual contributions are determined which will gradually accumulate a fund sufficient to provide each employee's pension at retirement. The amount of the pension benefit usually is related to the employee's compensation, years of service, or both.

With a defined contribution pension plan (also called a money purchase plan), the annual contribution to the employee's account is fixed or definitely determinable, and the employee receives whatever size retirement benefit can be purchased with the funds accumulated in the account. Usually, the annual contribution (which usually is paid throughout the year) is a fixed percentage of the employee's compensation. There are limits on the amount of contributions that can be made to a pension plan, whether the plan is a defined benefit or a defined contribution plan.

Contribution Limitations

The contribution limitation rules are complex but there are general rules which apply. With respect to defined benefit plans, the highest annual benefit payable must not exceed the lesser of (a) 100 percent of the participant's average compensation in his/her high three consecutive years of employment while a plan participant, or (b) $125,000, in 1997, as adjusted for inflation. (The maximum is indexed annually for inflation and changes only in increments of $5,000.)[6] The annual contribution limitation for defined contribution plans must not exceed the lesser of (a) 25 percent of the participant's compensation, or (b) $30,000 in 1997, as indexed for inflation. (This annual limit also is indexed for inflation and changes only in increments of $5,000.)[7] When an employer has more than one plan, as is often the case, the limitation rules are more complex and generally apply to all plans collectively.

As its name implies, a profit sharing plan is one for sharing employer profits with employees. A profit sharing plan need not provide a definite, predetermined formula for determining amounts of profits to be shared. But in the absence of a formula, there must be recurring and substantial contributions made on behalf of employees. However, there must be a definite, predetermined formula for allocating the contributions among the participants, and for distributing funds to the employees after the lapse of a fixed number of years, at retirement, at death, etc. The allocation formula generally is related to compensation, although service and other factors may be given consideration. Since the contributions are related to compensation, the defined contribution limitations above apply.

A stock bonus plan provides benefits similar to those of a profit sharing plan but the benefits are distributable in stock of the employer, and employer contributions are not necessarily dependent on profits. For the purpose of allocating contributions and distributing benefits, the plan is subject to the same requirements as a profit sharing plan.

Plan Requirements

In order to enjoy the tax advantages mentioned above, qualified plans must meet a set of requirements:

1. A plan must be established in the United States by an employer for the benefit of employees or their beneficiaries. Plan assets may not be used for any purpose other than for the exclusive benefit of employees or beneficiaries until all liabilities to those two groups have been satisfied.[8]

2. A plan must meet minimum age and service standards and minimum coverage requirements. The general minimum age and service standard is age 21, with one year of service; two years of service may be required if there is immediate 100 percent vesting.[9] The minimum coverage requirement will be met if the plan passes a ratio percentage test. Under this test, the percentage of nonhighly compensated employees who benefit under the plan must be at least 70 percent of the highly compensated employees who benefit under the plan.[10] There is also a minimum participation rule that applies only to defined benefit plans in years after December 31, 1996; before 1997 this rule applied to all plans.[11]

3. A plan must provide for contributions or benefits which are not discriminatory. There are three basic requirements: (a) contributions and benefits must not discriminate in favor of highly compensated employees; (b) benefits, rights and features must be made available to employees in a nondiscriminatory manner; and (c) the effect of plan amendments and plan terminations must be nondiscriminatory.[12]

4. Benefits and contribution amounts must not exceed the limitations mentioned above.[13]

5. A plan must provide for minimum vesting standards. Generally, an employee must be given nonforfeitable rights to accrued benefits derived from employer contributions in accordance with one of two vesting schedules: (a) five-year cliff vesting; an employee who has five years must have 100 percent vesting of accrued benefits; (b) 3/7 vesting; an employee who has at least three years of service must have vesting in 20 percent of accrued benefits, with the percentage graduating each year until there is 100 percent vesting after seven years.[14]

6.   A plan must provide for distributions to satisfy both the commencement rules and the minimum distribution rules. Unless the participant directs otherwise, distributions must commence within 60 days following the later of: (a) the close of the plan year of the earlier of normal retirement age under the plan or age 65; (b) the close of the plan year when the participant has 10 years of plan participation; or (c) the close of the plan year when the participant ceases employment.[15] The minimum distribution requirements are an interrelated set of rules which require that distributions from a plan must begin by a specific date and also that a participant's entire interest must be distributed within certain specified periods.[16]

7.   Certain plans must provide that unless waived by the participant, with the consent of his/her spouse, the automatic survivor benefit is a qualified joint and survivor annuity.[17]

Definition

8.   There must be provisions for actions to be taken should the plan become "top-heavy." A top-heavy plan is one where the benefits are disproportionately in favor of highly compensated and other key employees.[18]

9.   A plan must provide that benefits generally may not be assigned or alienated (transfer the ownership), or subject to garnishment or execution (a court order). One notable exception is the collection of federal taxes from benefits. Another is what is referred to as a "qualified domestic relations order."[19]

401(k) Plan

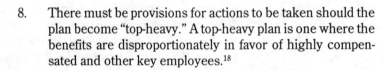

Definition

A 401(k) plan generally is a profit sharing or stock bonus plan (see above) which provides for contributions to be made pursuant to a "cash or deferred arrangement" (CODA) under which individual participants elect to take amounts in cash or to have the amounts deferred.[20] Amounts which are deferred are excluded from the participant's gross income in the year of deferral and treated as employer contributions. Thus, the deferrals are contributions made with before-tax dollars. Some plans call for all of the contributions to be from participant deferrals and others for some of the contributions to be ordinary employer contributions. The latter plans usually are referred to as matching since the scheme often involves the employer making contributions in amounts which are the same or a percentage of what the participant contributes.

The amount of elective deferrals an individual can exclude from income in a year is subject to a ceiling, which also applies collectively to other elective deferral plans such as tax deferred (or tax sheltered) annuities, in which the individual participates. The limit for tax years beginning in 1997 is $9,500; the limit is adjusted annually for inflation in increments of $500.[21]

In order to meet nondiscrimination requirements, 401(k) plans must either satisfy one of two actual deferral percentage (ADP) tests or be SIMPLE (Savings Incentive Match Plan for Employees) 401(k) plans (first available in 1997).(Beginning after 1998, an additional design-based safe harbor will be available.)[22] The two ADP tests are not so complex in themselves but they require relatively elaborate records and data and they compare the current year with the previous year. Then, if a violation is found, remedial action must be taken such as refunding contributions and correcting accounts and records. Many small employers do not have elaborate enough data processing systems or are not in a position to pay outside administrators the fees necessary to administer 401(k) plans, notwithstanding the great popularity of the plans among the public.

SIMPLE 401(k) Plans

Planning Tips

That is the reason that SIMPLE 401(k) plans were created. These plans are for employers with no more than 100 employees earning $5,000 or more in the preceding year. Employees must be permitted to elect to have the employer make elective contributions on behalf of employees, the amount being a percentage of compensation up to $6,000. The employer must match dollar-for-dollar up to 3 percent of compensation. Alternatively, the employer may elect to make nonelective contributions of 2 percent. All contributions are immediately vested in full.[23] By using this type of plan, the employer does not have to deal with the ADP testing of conventional 401(k) plans. As indicated, the SIMPLE 401(k) is a new creation. It remains to be seen how popular it will become.

To this point, we have looked broadly at plans for relatively large employers, with the possible exception of the SIMPLE 401(k). Before we turn to other tax-advantaged retirement plans, we should again state the rule of thumb that qualified retirement plans usually are better served by group annuities, with separate variable accounts, than by individual variable annuities. Many of the reasons were discussed in Chapter 7. Nonetheless, there are opportunities to use individual contracts even in connection with these larger plans.

Using Variable Annuities in Qualified Plans

In a number of cases, plan administrators are perfectly well equipped to provide complete service to participants of qualified plans while they are actively employed. However, when retirement time comes, different arrangements must be made. That is because these administrators are not in a position to administer all of the options the participant has under the law. They might be able easily to administer a life income of some kind but, perhaps, cannot administer periodic withdrawals at the participant's direction. They may not be well equipped to administer mandatory distributions, generally beginning at age 70½, should the participant want to leave a large portion of his/her account intact.

Planning Tips

These and other needs may necessitate the rolling over of the plan proceeds, on a tax free basis, to an individual variable annuity capable of handling all of the options available. Rollover distributions from qualified retirement plans may be made to either another qualified retirement plan or to an individual retirement plan. In the examples discussed just above, which pertain to plan proceeds at retirement, the usual choice is an individual retirement plan. The rules pertaining to rollovers after 1992 have been simplified; a most important one to note is that the rollover must be completed within 60 days after receipt of the distribution.[24]

The distribution can be placed in a variable annuity that is an individual retirement annuity (IRA). Then, the many options and procedures which are part of the variable annuity can be available. Of course, the IRA participant will need to keep in mind that his/her actions will be treated in accordance with the rules pertaining to IRAs. While this discussion has been concerned with actions at retirement time, there are reasons for rollovers to IRAs prior to retirement, the most common being a termination of employment with an employer which has a qualified retirement plan and new employment or self-employment without a plan to which to roll over a distribution. The IRA rollover distribution needs to be allocated to accounts and new contributions can be made in accordance with IRA rules.

Lump Sum Distributions

Sales Tips

A variable annuity also is a good place for a lump sum distribution from a qualified retirement plan. Certain people will determine it is best for them to pay the taxes on a lump sum distribution and save and invest the money on their own. A five-year averaging may be elected by certain people who take such distributions after age 59½[25]; this provision remains available until the end of 1999. Certain other people, born before 1936, are eligible for potentially more favorable tax treatment with some of the distribution being treated with a ten-year averaging and other of the distribution given long-term capital gains treatment.

Prior to 1997, large distributions (i.e., amounts in excess of $155,000, as indexed for 1996) from qualified retirement plans ordinarily were subject to a 15 percent penalty in addition to the ordinary income tax which, considering the amounts involved, would be at very high rates. This tax (as well as the corresponding excess accumulations tax) was repealed by The Taxpayer Relief Act of 1997, effective for distributions received (and decedents dying) after December 31, 1996.[26] Obviously, there will be considerable competition among financial services providers to accommodate the people who want to take distributions and put the money to work. A variable annuity is a good choice for many of the people who will elect to take distributions.

INDIVIDUAL RETIREMENT ANNUITIES

Many people use variable annuities in their individual retirement accounts or annuities (IRAs). IRAs are personal retirement plans, not dependent on an employer. An IRA also may be funded with mutual funds and other investments provided the arrangement is one which qualifies with IRA procedures. A disclosure statement, and a copy of the governing IRA instrument, must be furnished to the buyer at least seven days before the plan is established or purchased. That is why disclosure statements and related documents often are included in the prospectuses of variable annuities which may be used in IRAs. Earnings on the variable annuity inside the IRA accumulate with a deferral of income tax generally until the values are taken out. Of course, values in variable annuities, which are not in IRAs, also accumulate on a tax deferred basis.

Contributions

What makes the IRA different from nonqualified annuities is the fact that the individual may be able to take an income tax deduction on the contribution made. An individual, under age 70½ who has compensation of at least the amount being contributed, may be able to deduct up to $2,000 per year. A contribution also may be made for a non-working spouse. Beginning in 1997, the total for both spouses can be as much as $4,000; it had been $2,250 in prior years. When both spouses are working and earning at least $2,000 each, the total for the two remains $4,000.[27]

Reminder

The deduction for contributions made to individual and spousal plans may be reduced or eliminated if the contributing individual or the spouse is an "active participant" in a qualified retirement plan. In 1998 a phase out of the deduction begins at $30,000 of adjusted gross income (AGI) for an individual and $50,000 for a married couple filing jointly. This amount increases each year as shown below.[28] Thus, many persons who participate in qualified plans do not have IRAs available on a deductible basis. Financial services products may be purchased to fund IRAs on a nondeductible basis. However, when annuities, including variable annuities, are to be used, there appear to be few advantages to nondeductible IRAs that annuities do not already have. (One exception to this generalization is the Roth IRA, created by The Taxpayer Relief Act of 1997, from which tax-free distributions may be received under certain circumstances.[29] Further, some of the formalities and limitations of nondeductible IRAs do not apply to annuities when they are not in plans.

Single Taxpayer

For taxable years beginning in:	The applicable dollar amount is:
1998	$30,000
1999	$31,000
2000	$32,000
2001	$33,000
2002	$34,000
2003	$40,000
2004	$45,000
2005 and after	$50,000

Married Taxpayers Filing a Joint Return

For taxable years beginning in:	The applicable dollar amount is:
1998	$50,000
1999	$51,000
2000	$52,000
2001	$53,000
2002	$54,000
2003	$60,000
2004	$65,000
2005	$70,000
2006	$75,000
2007 and later	$80,000

Distributions

One of the limitations does apply to annuities as discussed in Chapter 12. Amounts distributed from a regular or spousal IRA, to the individual for whom the plan is maintained, before the person reaches age 59½ are premature distributions and subject to an additional tax of 10 percent of the amount includable in gross income. The penalty does not apply to distributions:

1. made to a beneficiary, or the individual's estate, on or after the death of the individual;

2. attributable to the individual's disability;

3. which are part of a series of substantially equal periodic payments made (at least annually) for the life or life expectancy of the individual, or the joint lives or joint life expectancy of the individual and his/her designated beneficiary;

4. made after 1996 for medical care but only to the extent allowable as a medical expense deduction during the year.[30]

Of more importance to most IRA participants are the minimum distribution rules. Distributions from a traditional IRA must begin by

April 1 of the year after the year in which the owner reaches 70½, whether or not the owner has retired. At a minimum, the balance must be distributed over one of the following periods:

1. the life of the owner;

2. the lives of the owner and a designated beneficiary; or

3. a fixed period or period certain not extending beyond the life expectancy of the owner (or the joint life and last survivor expectancy of the owner and designated beneficiary).

When a fixed period is used, the minimum amount required is determined separately each year using one of two methods. Distributions made during the life of the owner must also comply with an incidental death benefit rule. This amount may be greater than the amount required to be distributed under the regular rule. The regular rule alone is used when the only beneficiary is the owner's spouse.

Rules apply to distributions made on account of the death of the owner from both the traditional IRAs and the Roth IRAs. If the owner dies after distributions have begun, but before the entire interest has been paid, the balance generally must be distributed at least as rapidly as under the method in effect as of the owner's death. If the owner dies before distributions have begun, the entire interest must be distributed by the end of five calendar years following the owner's death, unless a beneficiary has been designated. Then the payments can extend over the beneficiary's life or for a period at least as long as the beneficiary's life expectancy, providing the payments commence by the end of the year following the owner's death. When the beneficiary is the owner's surviving spouse, distributions can commence at the end of the year the owner would have been 70½, if that is later.

Whether the owner dies before or after distributions have begun, the surviving spouse, if a beneficiary, may elect to treat the entire account or annuity as the surviving spouse's own plan. The surviving spouse may make contributions to it and make rollovers from it.[31]

Caution

The reason it is so important to comply with the minimum distribution rules is the tax assessed in the event of a shortfall. If the amount distributed from an IRA is less than the minimum required distribution for the year, there is an excise tax equal to 50 percent of the amount by which the distribution made in the calendar year falls short of the required amount. That is a stiff penalty to be avoided. As indicated elsewhere, variable annuity issuers who provide annuities for IRAs usually are equipped to handle minimum distributions adequately enough to avoid running afoul of the minimum distribution rules.

SIMPLE IRA

A small employer (one with no more than 100 employees who received at least $5,000 of compensation for the preceding year) may set up a SIMPLE (Savings Incentive Match Plan for Employees) IRA plan. These plans resemble the SIMPLE 401(k) plans mentioned above in many ways. SIMPLE IRAs are salary reduction arrangements where employees may elect to receive payments in cash or contribute them to the plan. Contributions are expressed as a percentage of compensation and may not exceed $6,000 per year. The employer must match or make nonelective contributions. The match formula is dollar-for-dollar up to 3 percent of compensation; however a special rule permits the employer to elect a lower percentage (not less than 1 percent). The employer may not use the lower percentage if the election would result in the percentage being lower than 3 percent in more than two out of five years. The nonelective employer contribution alternative is 2 percent of compensation for each employee who earned at least $5,000 in any 2 preceding years and is reasonably expected to receive at least $5,000 during the year. All contributions to a SIMPLE IRA must be fully vested and may not be subject to any prohibition on withdrawals, nor conditioned on their retention in the account. However, the premature distribution penalty for withdrawals is increased from 10 percent to 25 percent during the first two years of participation. Contributions are excludable from the employee's income.[32]

Simplified Employee Pension

Definition

A simplified employee pension (SEP) is an individual retirement account or annuity which may accept an expanded rate of contributions from employers. The employer must contribute for every employee who is 21 years of age, has performed services for the employer during the year and for at least three of the past five years and who has received at least $400 (in 1997 indexed) in compensation from the employer for the year. Employer contributions must be determined under a definite written allocation formula, must not discriminate in favor of the highly compensated and must bear a uniform relationship to compensation. Contributions cannot be conditioned on keeping them in the plan and the employer may not prohibit withdrawals. IRA withdrawal rules apply. Contributions may not exceed 15 percent of compensation (after reduction by the contribution itself), with a maximum of $24,000 (in 1997 indexed).[33] Thus, a SEP is a good way for a very small employer, even one self-employed person, to set up a plan and make deductible contributions at the higher limits. Variable annuities can be used effectively to fund a SEP.

A SAR-SEP is a simplified employee pension offered on a salary reduction basis. No new SAR-SEPs may be established after 1996. However, plans established prior to 1997 may continue to operate, receive contributions, and add new employees.[34] Small employers interested in salary reduction arrangements may turn to SIMPLE IRAs or possibly to SIMPLE 401(k) plans. Small employers also may facilitate their employees setting up their own IRAs by providing for payroll deduction. The potential availability of deductible contributions of up to $4,000 total for a husband and wife makes IRAs more worthwhile than ever. In addition, employers can facilitate saving and investing on a nonqualified basis by providing for payroll deduction for purchases of variable and fixed annuities and life, disability income and other types of insurance and savings products.

TAX SHELTERED ANNUITIES

Tax sheltered annuities (also referred to as tax deferred annuities, although the latter term also is used to describe nonqualified annuities) are available to employees of organizations which are either tax exempt as described in Code Section 501(c)(3) or a public school system.[35] Many variable annuities are purchased by these employees, especially school teachers and hospital employees including a number of highly paid professional medical staff members. Many registered representatives concentrate on marketing these annuities almost exclusively. Products other than annuities also can be used.

TSAs usually are purchased by employees through their employer on a salary reduction basis by payroll deduction. The employer collects the contributions and remits them to the insurance company or other product issuer. The maximum amount of salary reduction eligible is determined by calculating an exclusion allowance using relatively complex formulas beginning with 20 percent of compensation. Formulas can take past service into consideration, thereby increasing what otherwise could be contributed. Further, the allowance can be calculated so that a level contribution can be made. The allowance must consider contributions to other plans, such as state teacher retirement plans.[36] The overall limits (lesser of 25 percent of compensation or $30,000, indexed) of qualified plans apply.[37]

Most of the provisions of other plans discussed above also apply to TSAs. There are provisions for employer contributions and matching but matching contributions are not common among plans involving teachers and hospital employees. Nondiscrimination rules apply when there are employer contributions, of course, and, to a lesser extent, to salary reduction contributions. The 10 percent penalty for distributions made before age 59½ applies with most of the same exceptions. There is an additional exception for an employee who separates from service after attaining age 55.[38] It is more common for employees to borrow from their plans than for them to take premature distributions. On the other hand, the loan is treated as a premature distribution if it is not repaid within five years. However, a loan used to acquire a dwelling that within a reasonable time is to be used as the participant's principal residence is not subject to the five-year repayment provision.[39] Minimum distributions are required to begin by April 1 of the year following the year in which the taxpayer turns age 70½ or retires, whichever is later.[40]

NONQUALIFIED RETIREMENT PLANS

Some employees, especially the more highly compensated, need to have more retirement income than can be provided through qualified retirement plans. These plans, plus social security benefits, total a smaller percentage of higher paid employees' working years income, because of the caps on social security retirement contributions and resulting benefits. To add to the retirement incomes of such employees, employers turn to nonqualified retirement plans such as supplemental retirement, deferred compensation, and employee bonus arrangements.

Supplemental retirement plans and deferred compensations plans (these terms sometimes are used interchangeably) operate in much the same way. An employer (for this discussion a regular C corporation) sets up a plan whereby either the employer makes contributions in addition to usual compensation (a supplemental retirement plan) or the employee forgoes or reduces compensation and has the employer make contributions (a deferred compensation plan). Since the arrangement is not a qualified retirement plan, contributions are not deductible currently but they are not included in the employee's current income because under the terms of the plan, his/her rights are both nontransferable and subject to a substantial risk of forfeiture.[41] This usually means that the employer owns the financial services product into which contributions will be made.

At a later time — at retirement or other time in the future, or at the employee's death prior to retirement — supplemental or deferred compensation is paid out. At that time, the employer is entitled to take a deduction for amounts attributable to prior contributions which are paid to the employee. The employee includes those amounts as income.[42] Thus, the employee has postponed tax on the amounts until retirement when, presumably, he/she is in a lower income tax bracket. The employer did not get deductions over the years as contributions were made but does get deductions as amounts are paid out — better late than never. And besides, since this has been a plan for the more highly compensated, a group which may include the principals of the business, it is an incentive for those most valuable to the success of the business.

If the employer is going to make contributions over the years, and in that way informally fund the plan so that the needed money is most likely to be in place, the contributions will go to purchase a product or products. If the contributions are used to purchase variable or fixed annuities, the "nonnatural person" rule comes into play. When an

Reminder

annuity contract is owned by a corporation, partnership, or trust, "the income on the contract," (essentially the gain each year over the premiums paid) is taxable. (See Chapter 12 for further discussion of this rule.)

Though the rule with respect to annuities was different some years back, the nonnatural person rule puts annuities in a position similar to most other products. Life insurance stands pretty much alone as a product where the earnings are deferred into the future; where life insurance is appropriate to provide the informal funding, it should be considered. But if life insurance is not appropriate, for whatever reason, one should do the calculations, compare annuities with other products, especially giving weight to the income options, and choose the best product for informal funding.

BONUS PLANS

So-called bonus plans for providing supplemental retirement benefits operate differently. Here, the employer (a C corporation) arranges to provide increased compensation, a "bonus," to the employee so that he/she may purchase a product to fund supplemental benefits. The additional compensation is a currently deductible business expense for the employer, provided that the employee's total compensation is a reasonable amount,[43] and the employee includes it as additional income. Sometimes, the employer advances an additional amount that is sufficient for the employee to pay the income tax on the increased compensation thereby maintaining the employee's take home pay. This arrangement is sometimes referred to as a "double bonus" plan.

The employee owns the annuity or other financial product and, as a result, there are no restrictions on what he/she can do with it. For that reason, bonus plans are offered to only the most valuable of employees, including the principals of the business who are employees. The "nonnatural person" rule does not apply to a variable or fixed annuity purchased by the employee because a natural person owns it. And a variable annuity is a most effective way of providing supplemental retirement income.

The supplemental retirement, deferred compensation and employee bonus plans we have discussed here are in their most straightforward form. There are a great many variations of them, including the use of several kinds of trusts, to effect some measure of security from the creditors of the corporation and to impose at least some restrictions on the rights of either the employer or employee, depending on the type of plan. These variations are beyond the scope of this book.

EDUCATION FUNDING

The education of children is one of the major reasons listed for accumulating money. The cost of education continues to rise faster than the overall rate of inflation so that today's college costs, high as they are, will be exceeded by costs in the future. And people's ability to pay continues to decline. At the same time, the gulf in earnings between those with college educations and those without is widening. Clearly, saving and investing in advance is called for.

Variable annuities can play a significant role in accumulating money for college. But things are not as simple as merely saving money and then using it, as with a savings account. A parent who purchases a variable annuity when his/her son or daughter is young can pay continuing premiums into a variable account, engage in dollar cost averaging, and accumulate a substantial sum by the time the child is ready for college. During the accumulation years, earnings on the savings and investments have been deferred so that the parent was not required to reduce payments somewhat in order to also pay income tax on the earnings each year.

If the parent has reached the age of 59½ by the time he/she needs to take withdrawals, income tax will be limited to the parent's rate on the amount withdrawn (until all of the earnings have been withdrawn, after which the remaining amounts may be withdrawn without tax). If the parent withdraws prior to age 59½, the 10 percent penalty on premature distributions applies.[44] This very well may be a disadvantage but someone in that position should do the tax calculation to be sure how disadvantageous it is. We always like to assume our customers will have high incomes when their children are ready for college, but some will not. Someone who has bought a variable annuity primarily for retirement, and then is confronted with higher college costs than anticipated, may have to turn to his/her variable annuity. The tax cost, including the penalty, may be worth incurring in such a situation.

A parent who is several years away from age 59½, at the time of college expenses, may make delayed use of a variable annuity. The parent may be willing to borrow, using a second mortgage credit line for example, to pay the major costs of college knowing full well that he/she can take withdrawals without a penalty in a few years and pay off the second mortgage balance. Interest on the second mortgage credit line loan usually has been deductible. The calculation of the cost of the whole process takes several steps, taking into account deferral of tax on the variable annuity earnings, deductibility of the mortgage interest, and tax on the withdrawals (but no penalty tax). Further, if the variable annuity is inside an IRA, distributions to pay for certain education expenses are not subject to the 10 percent penalty. (See Chapter 4.)

It often is grandparents who fund a major portion of their grandchildren's college expenses. When a grandparent purchases a variable annuity, the same deferral of taxes on the earnings occurs. When the grandchild reaches college age, the grandparent is over age 59½ and can make withdrawals without penalty. Presumably, the grandparent is in a lower tax bracket than when the earnings deferrals were taking place while the grandparent was working. The grandparent pays the tax on the withdrawals and gives them to the parents or grandchildren for college expenses. In this case, the grandparent is in control of whom is to receive the money; should the grandchild not be a good college candidate or one or both of the parents not be as dependable as the grandparent would like to see, the grandparent can act accordingly.

Note that when the grandparent gives money for college to either the parent or grandchild, the gift is subject to the federal gift tax. However, a gift equal to the annual exclusion amount ($10,000 in 1997) may be given each year to any number of recipients without a gift tax being payable. And if both grandparent-spouses join in the gift an amount equal to twice the annual exclusion amount may be given to each recipient without gift tax.[45] When there are several grandchildren and two parents, there are quite a few recipients. Obviously, a variable annuity can work very well in that situation.

GIFTS OF ANNUITIES

From time to time a family member will want to give a financial asset to another family member. He/she may want to do so either to help the other family member financially or so that the asset is removed from the estate of the owner for federal estate tax purposes, or for both reasons. When the gift is to be of an annuity issued after April 22, 1987, things can be a little more complicated. The annuity owner has two choices: surrender the annuity and make a gift of the cash or make a gift of the annuity itself.

If the owner surrenders the annuity contract, the income tax on the gain in the contract must be paid. Further, if the owner is under age 59½, a 10 percent penalty applies to the amount subject to tax. Gifts of the cash are subject to gift tax, as just above, with the availability of the annual gift tax exclusion of $10,000 per recipient.

The second choice is to make a gift of the annuity. However, in such a case, the person making the gift is treated as having received an amount equal to the gain in the contract for income tax purposes.[46] The donee of the gift of the annuity receives a contract where the investment in the contract now includes all of the previous gain. Therefore, future gain will be calculated from this higher starting point and income tax deferral of earnings goes on. The gift of the annuity is subject to the gift tax. The value above the annual exclusion amount ($10,000 or $20,000 if the owner-donor and spouse join in the gift) will require a gift tax to be paid unless a portion of the donor's unified estate and gift tax credit is used. Again, careful consideration and a series of calculations are necessary in deciding which way, if either, to go.

GIFTS TO CHARITY

Considerable use is made of annuities in estate planning, especially planning involving gifts to charity in one form or another. For the most part, however, these are not commercial annuities, the subject of this book. Here, the dictionary definition of annuity is applicable: a payment of a fixed sum of money at regular intervals of time, especially yearly (annual and annuity are from the same root). We will briefly review some of these charitable gift planning techniques.

There are several overriding considerations in charitable gift planning. One is to reduce the size of a person's estate, for federal estate tax purposes, and at the same time make a gift to a charity the donor is interested in supporting. Another is to reduce current income taxes somewhat by making the gift. A third is to not necessarily give up all of the benefit of the property being given during the lifetime of the donor or one or more of his/her beneficiaries. Quite frequently, the property to be given has appreciated significantly in value and would be subject to a substantial capital gain tax if sold by the donor instead of being given away. Assuming the charity to which the property is being given is an exempt organization under Code section 170(c) it will not be subject to income tax if the property is sold for cash.

Definition

An individual may enter into a charitable gift annuity arrangement. This is an agreement between a charity and the person whereby the person donates property in exchange for an annuity to be paid by the charity for the person's life. A commercial annuity could be used but usually is not because the charity wants to make immediate use of the property or sell it and put the sale proceeds to use. The annuity payments are made directly from the charity and backed by the charity's assets and good name. Obviously, one would want to enter into such an arrangement only with a charity in a position to make good on the lifetime income commitment.

CHARITABLE TRUSTS

An often used charitable gift planning arrangement is the charitable remainder trust (CRT). A CRT involves an irrevocable gift in trust to a charity with payments continuing to a noncharitable beneficiary for life or for a term of years. At the death of the individual or at the end of the term of years, the property remaining in the trust, the remainder interest, becomes the property of the charity. There is a minimum (5 percent) which must be paid out of the trust each year, as well as a maximum permitted payout of 50% (beginning with transfers after June 18, 1997). Furthermore, the value of the remainder interest must be at least 10% of the initial net fair market value of the property placed in the trust (for transfers made after July 28, 1997). The requirements for setting up a CRT are complex[47] but charities which attract a number of these gifts (e.g., colleges and community and arts organizations) have put together standardized procedures for implementing them. If certain requirements are met, the gift of the property can result in an immediate income tax charitable deduction for the donor.[48]

There are two types of CRTs: the charitable remainder annuity trust and the charitable remainder unitrust. The annuity trust provides for a fixed payment of at least 5 percent and not more than 50% of the trust's fair market value at inception. Additional gifts to the trust may not be made. The unitrust provides for a variable amount to be paid to the noncharitable beneficiary. The percentage (at least 5 percent and not more than 50%) to be paid is fixed but the assets in the trust are valued annually resulting in possible variable payments. A unitrust may be designed to pay out only the net income of the trust.

In recent years, CRTs have been combined with what is referred to as a "wealth replacement trust," actually an irrevocable trust funded with life insurance. Typically, an individual gives appreciated property in trust to a charity with the individual retaining a life income from the property value. The wealth replacement trust purchases a life insurance policy on the donor, payable to the donor's beneficiaries, usually family members. Because of income tax savings resulting from the charitable gift deduction, dollars presumably are available with which to pay life insurance premiums. When the donor dies, the remainder interest goes to the charity and the beneficiaries receive life insurance proceeds. These are happy results when the arrangements have been designed properly.

With a charitable lead trust, the income and remainder roles are reversed. Under the trust, the charity receives the income (lead) interest and the remainder interest comes back to the donor or his/ her beneficiaries at death or after a term of years. The lead trust must pay income in the form of either a guaranteed interest or a unitrust interest. The guaranteed interest is of a fixed amount; the unitrust interest is of a fixed percentage of the value of the property in the trust.[49]

Finally, there is the "pooled income fund." Donors make gifts of property which are placed in a pool. Each donor names a beneficiary to receive income from the fund, often for the life of the beneficiary. The amount of income generally is determined by the earnings of the fund. The charity receives the remainder interest in the property.

CHAPTER FOOTNOTES

1. IRC Sections 402(a), 403(a), 404.

2. IRC Sections 402(a), 403(a).

3. IRC Section 402.

4. IRC Sections 72, 402(a), 403(a).

5. IRC Section 501.

6. IRC Section 415(b).

7. IRC Section 415(c).

8. IRC Section 401(a).

9. IRC Sections 401(a)(3), 410(a)(1).

10. Reg. §§1.410(b)-2(b)(2)(i).

11. IRC Section 401(a)(26).

12. IRC Section 401(a)(4).

13. IRC Section 415.

14. IRC Section 401(a)(7).

15. IRC Section 401(a)(14).

16. IRC Section 401(a)(9).

17. IRC Section 401(a)(11).

18. IRC Section 416.

19. IRC Section 401(a)(13).

20. IRC Section 401(k).

21. IRC Section 402(g).

22. IRC Sections 401(k)(3), 401(k)(11), 401(k)(12).

23. IRC Section 401(k)(11).

24. IRC Section 402(c)(3).

25. IRC Section 402(d)(4)(B).

26. IRC Section 4980A, as repealed by TRA '97.

27. IRC Sections 219(b), 219(c).

28. IRC Section 219(g)(3)(B), as amended by TRA '97.

29. IRC Section 408A(d), as added by TRA '97.

30. IRC Section 72(t).

31. Prop. Reg. §§1.401(a)(9)-1, 1.401(a)(9)-2, 1,408-8.

32. IRC Sections 408(p), 72(t).

33. IRC Section 408(k).

34. IRC Section 408(k)(6).

35. IRC Section 403(b).

36. IRC Section 403(b)(2)

37. IRC Section 415(a)(2).

38. IRC Section 72(t)(2)(A)(v).

39. IRC Section 72(p).

40. IRC Section 401(a)(9).

41. IRC Sections 402(b)(1), 403(c), 83(a).

42. IRC Section 404(a)(5).

43. IRC Section 162(a).

44. IRC Section 72(q).

45. IRC Section 2503(b).

46. IRC Section 72(e)(4)(C).

47. Generally IRC Sections 170, 664.

48. IRC Sections 170(f)(2)(B), 664(d).

49. IRC Section 170(f)(2)(B).

12

TAXATION OF VARIABLE ANNUITIES

FEDERAL INCOME TAX

Because annuities, including variable annuities, accumulate substantial amounts of money which are withdrawn and/or distributed in the future, their income tax aspects are of importance. So, too, are their estate tax and gift tax aspects. In this discussion, we will look at the principal provisions of the federal tax laws affecting annuities. Annuities also may be subject to applicable state income, gift and estate or inheritance tax laws. In most instances, federal taxes are considerably more substantial and, therefore more important, but state taxes should be taken into account.

In Chapter 11, we consider annuities that are part of qualified retirement plans. These annuity premiums, which are plan contributions, usually are tax deductible. That is not the case with respect to annuities purchased outside of these plans. The general rule is that these premiums, whether paid on a single premium basis or on a periodic premium basis are non-deductible. As we shall see, these non-deductible premiums are the basis for determining what is referred to as the investment in the contract, the amount which the owner may receive without any further income tax.

The interest or earnings credited to an annuity, which meet conditions of the Internal Revenue Code,[1] are not taxed at the time they are credited provided that they remain inside the contract and are not withdrawn or distributed. As we see in Chapter 11, this statement is generally true today only so long as the owner of the annuity contract is a natural person. If premiums are paid after February 28, 1986 into a deferred annuity contract owned by a corporation or other entity not considered to be a natural person under the law, the interest or earnings credited each year are taxable currently.[2] To be more precise, the amount to be taxed is calculated by taking the sum of the net surrender value at the end of the taxable year and any amounts distributed during the taxable year and prior taxable years. From this amount is subtracted the sum of the net premiums for the current and prior taxable years and any amounts included in gross income for prior taxable years (presumably amounts withdrawn).[3]

The nonnatural person rule does not apply to annuities held by qualified retirement plans, IRAs, tax sheltered annuities, single premium immediate annuities, and damage award payouts. When an annuity contract is held by a trust, corporation, or other nonnatural person acting as an agent for a natural person, interest and earnings credited are income tax-deferred.[4] The place where this latter provision applies most frequently is trusts. Generally, the IRS has indicated that it views most types of trusts that have natural persons as beneficiaries to be acting as agents for the natural persons.

Reminder

Note that the nonnatural person rule is directed at annuities where premiums have been paid after February 28, 1986. Thus, if all premiums were paid after that date, the rule clearly applies. Just as clearly, it does not appear to apply where all premiums were paid before that date. When some were paid before and some after, things are not so clear. It would not be a good practice to subject a customer to this possibility if it can be avoided by not involving a nonnatural person. Finally, there is no doubt that the rule applies to annuity contracts purchased today.

WITHDRAWALS

Caution

When money is withdrawn from an annuity, as either a partial withdrawal or partial surrender, there is an income tax to be considered. There also may be a 10 percent penalty tax for a premature distribution in some instances. In addition, there may be a surrender charge applicable. The applicability and workings of the surrender charge are discussed in Chapter 8. But since the surrender charge and particularly the penalty tax are sometimes confused, we mention the surrender charge here. If the surrender charge applies because the amount surrendered is in excess of the surrender-charge-free amount permitted under the contract and because the applicable surrender charge period has not run, the charge will be levied against the amount being withdrawn. This has no effect on whether the penalty tax applies.

Before we consider the penalty tax further, let us look at taxation of the withdrawal itself. If the annuity was entered into after August 13, 1982, the current rule referred to as the "interest first" rule applies. If the contract was entered into before August 14, 1982, the old rule referred to as the "cost recovery rule" applies. Since the old rule is more favorable when there are withdrawals, an important point is to attempt to preserve its applicability when changes, particularly tax-free exchanges, are made to old contracts. We will look at this point later in this chapter.

Under the interest first rule, amounts received are taxable as income to the extent that the cash value of the contract immediately before the partial withdrawal or surrender exceeds the investment in the contract.[5] The investment in the contract, paid with previously taxed money, is then received without tax. Thus, all interest and earnings are distributed before any of the investment in the contract. As a result, when an annuity owner makes a series of withdrawals, the withdrawals are fully taxable until all of the interest and earnings have been distributed.

Under the cost recovery rule, the owner receives first whatever investment in the contract he/she has paid before August 14, 1982, which has been taxed previously, on a tax-free basis. Withdrawals of amounts which are the investment in the contract continue on a tax-free basis until all of that amount has been recovered. Interest and earnings are taxed only after the recovery of the investment (cost) paid before the 1982 date.[6]

The reason that this portion of the law was changed was to limit the tax advantages of deferred annuities to long range investment purposes. Congress was persuaded that the advantage of tax deferral of buildup in values of annuities should not be coupled with the further advantage of being able to withdraw at will with no tax payable until all of the investment in the contract had first been withdrawn. Other savings and investment products did not enjoy both of these advantages. (But note that partial surrenders of the cash values of life insurance generally still are governed by the cost recovery rule.)

An annuity entered into before August 14, 1982 may have some of its premiums paid before the rule change and some of them afterward. In such a case, amounts withdrawn are allocable first to investments made prior to August 14, 1982, then to income from those investments, then to income from investments made after August 13, and finally to investments in the contract made after August 13.[7] In other words, the sequence is tax-free, then fully taxed, then fully taxed, and then tax-free.

Planning Tips

A related consideration has to do with when an annuity, subject to the cost recovery rule, is involved in a tax-free exchange under Internal Revenue Code Section 1035 (the provisions of which we will take up shortly). Such a replacement contract succeeds to the status of the surrendered contract, for purposes of determining when amounts are to be considered invested in the contract and for computing the taxability of any withdrawals.[8] Investment in the replacement contract is considered made on, before or after August 13, 1982 to the same extent the investment was made on, before or after August 13 in the replaced contract.

PREMATURE DISTRIBUTIONS

Example

With respect to nonqualified annuities, the 10 percent penalty is applied to that portion of the distribution or withdrawal that is includable in income. If there is a substantial distribution, e.g., $50,000, and only a portion of it is subject to tax, e.g., $30,000, then the penalty applies to the $30,000 and amounts to $3,000. Of course, the $30,000 also is taxed at the taxpayer's marginal rate for the year of the distribution. When an annuity owner takes relatively smaller withdrawals, it may be the case that all of the amount withdrawn each year is subject to the penalty tax because all of the withdrawal is allocable to interest and earnings and none to the investment in the contract.

In addition to distributions from qualified plans, tax sheltered annuities and IRAs, the nonqualified annuity penalty tax does not apply to a distribution:

1. made after the taxpayer reaches age 59½;

2. attributable to the taxpayer's disability;

3. allocable to investment in the contract before August 14, 1982, including earnings on pre-August 14 investment;

4. made after the death of the annuity holder;

5. made under an immediate annuity contract;

6. made from an annuity purchased and held by an employer upon the termination of a qualified retirement plan;

7. under a qualified funding asset (i.e., any annuity contract which is purchased as a result of a liability to pay for damages which resulted from physical injury or sickness); or

8. which is part of a series of substantially equal periodic payments made (not less frequently than annually) for the life or life expectancy of the taxpayer or the joint lives or joint life expectancies of the taxpayer and his/her designated beneficiary.[9]

When the interest first rule and the 10 percent penalty became law, it did not take practitioners long to reason that if their customers bought several annuities, instead of just one, they could ameliorate some of the effects of the new rules by taking substantial or complete surrenders from one of them, leaving the others accumulating interest and earnings. Then, only part of the money would be subject to tax and the penalty, and the rest of the money could be recovered without tax or penalty. Since that was not the intention of the changes in the law, there is a further provision that all annuity contracts entered into after October 21, 1988, which are issued by the same company to the same policyholder during any calendar year, will be treated as one annuity contract for purposes of determining the amount of any distribution that is includable in income.[10] Again, this provision does not apply to qualified retirement plans, TSAs, IRAs, and immediate annuities.

Reminder

Before leaving this discussion of premature distributions, it is helpful to remember that qualified retirement plans have their own rules with respect to premature distributions as do IRAs. These rules are discussed in Chapter 11.

SECTION 1035 EXCHANGES

Planning Tips

Variable annuity owners sometimes want to "trade in" their contracts for newer ones because of interest rates on the guaranteed account, because of services or types of investments available with a new contract, because of insurance company solvency concerns (although this is a lesser consideration for variable annuities than for fixed annuities), and for other reasons. As noted earlier in this book, it is the position of regulators that exchanges of one variable annuity for another rarely is justified. That is because the advantages of new contracts seldom outweigh the costs, particularly the imposition of new surrender charge periods. However, there are times when exchanges are justified and there are numerous times when exchanges of life insurance policies and fixed annuities for variable annuities can be justified.

The reason the owner of a life insurance policy or annuity contract would want to make an exchange, instead of merely cashing in one contract and purchasing another, is so that there will be no taxable event at the time of the exchange. That is, there will be no inclusion of income subject to income tax. Tax-free exchanges of annuity and life insurance contracts are controlled by Internal Revenue Code Section 1035. That section says that the following exchanges may be made without current income taxation:

1. an annuity contract for another annuity contract;

2. a life insurance policy for an annuity contract;

3. an endowment contract for an annuity contract;

4. a life insurance policy for another life insurance policy;

5. a life insurance policy for an endowment contract; and

6.   an endowment contract for an endowment contract which will begin making payments no later than payments would have commenced under the old contract.

Note that there is no provision for exchanging an annuity contract for a life insurance policy. Generally, there can be no exchange which postpones further the event of taxation with respect to the contract. Note also that the two provisions involving endowment contracts have been reduced in significance because current Code definitions of life insurance make new endowment policies difficult to design. Here, again, we should point out that Section 1035 does not apply to qualified retirement plans, IRAs, and TSAs which have their own rollover provisions.

If an annuity is to be exchanged for another annuity, both contracts must be payable to the same person or persons to qualify under Section 1035.[11] The new contract can be issued by the same company or a different company.[12]

After a Section 1035 exchange, the cost basis (what has been referred to here as the investment in the annuity contract) of the new contract usually is the same as the old one. And in applicable cases, the cost recovery rule has been preserved, as discussed earlier in this chapter. The cost basis will not be the same if the annuity owner has received some cash in connection with the exchange. In that event, any gain, referred to as "boot," is recognized for income tax purposes.[13]

Caution

Further, if the exchanged contract has a loan outstanding, the situation may be complicated.[14] Since annuities usually do not have loans (partial withdrawals generally have been used instead), they are not a big issue. However, loans against life insurance policies can be an imposing problem. If a loan is merely erased during the exchange, the cash value securing the loan is considered to have been distributed and may result in a gain subject to current income tax. One should proceed cautiously when considering an exchange involving a life insurance policy with a large loan outstanding.

COMPLETE SURRENDERS

When an annuity owner surrenders the annuity in full, and does not elect to take payout provisions (to be discussed shortly), the owner must include in income for the year the difference between what he/she has received and the contract's cost basis (or investment in the contract).

In most instances, the cost basis is the premiums paid; however, there will be reductions in the basis for any distributions which have not been included in income. For example, if the owner has taken partial surrenders, some of which were not includable in income because of operation of the cost recovery rule or because all of the interest and earnings had been distributed first under the interest first rule, the cost basis will be reduced by the amount of the nonincludable distributions. Also, if the annuity contract is one that has paid dividends, the dividends are considered return of premiums. The return of premium is not subject to tax but it reduces the cost basis or investment in the contract. Once the cost basis of the contract has been determined, the full surrender is taxed under the cost recovery rule.[15] The gain is ordinary income, not capital gains.

SALE OF AN ANNUITY

Since an annuity is a piece of property, it can be sold. Generally, when there is a sale, the owner is taxed in the same way as when there has been a complete surrender. If the sale occurs after the owner has begun payout provisions (which we will take up next) the cost basis is adjusted for those amounts that have been received but were not includable in income. Apparently, if the sale has resulted in a loss, because the sale proceeds are less than the cost basis, the owner will have realized an ordinary loss. Such losses generally may not be deducted by individuals who entered into the annuity contract for personal reasons but may be claimed in connection with the owner's trade or business in a transaction entered into for profit.[16] If the new owner elects to take payout provisions, the payments will be taxed in the same way they would have been had the original owner retained the contract, except that they will be calculated with the new owner's life expectancy, etc. If the new owner is a corporation or other nonnatural person, those provisions will apply to annual increases in the contract values.

TAXATION OF PAYOUTS

As discussed in Chapter 7, a variable annuity owner may elect a fixed payout or a variable payout, with a number of options available with either of the two. Income taxation of the payout depends on which of the two has been selected although the principles involved are quite similar. The basic rule is that the purchaser is to receive the investment in the contract in equal tax-free installments over the payment period. The rest of the amount received each year is to be included in gross income. Thus, each payment is taxable in part and tax-free in part.

Fixed Payout

With respect to a fixed payout, the determination of what portion is taxed and what portion is not taxed is made using an exclusion ratio, which may be expressed as a fraction or as a percentage. It is arrived at by dividing the investment in the contract by the expected return. The exclusion ratio, so calculated, is applied to each annuity payment to find the portion that is excludable; then, the balance is includable in the year it is received.[17]

Example

To illustrate, let us use an uncomplicated example: a single life (a male), age 65, with no term certain or refund feature. Let us suppose that the life income to be paid is $750 per month, $9,000 per year, and that the investment in the contract has been $100,000. The numerator for the exclusion ratio is the $100,000 investment in the contract; the denominator is found by multiplying the annual return of $9,000 by 20, the unisex expected return multiple at age 65 in Table V of the IRS actuarial tables for taxing annuities; that figure is $180,000. When $100,000 is divided by $180,000, the result is 55.55 percent, the percentage of each year's payment that is excludable from income, approximately $5,000. The remainder, $4000, is to be received as previously taxed income.

If our example had been a fixed period or fixed amount, the denominator would be found by multiplying the annual return by the known number of years and months. The division of the investment in the contract by that expected return would result in a percentage of each year's payment which would be excludable from income, with the balance of the yearly payment includable.

In the case of joint life annuities, there are IRS actuarial tables indicating expectancy multiples; here, it depends on whether the payments will continue to the second annuitant (joint and survivor) or end when the first of the joint annuitants dies. When there is a term certain guarantee or a refund to a beneficiary, there are tables which establish percentages depending on the age of the annuitant. The applicable percentage is applied as a reduction in the investment in the contract.

Variable Payout

Example

When there is to be a variable payout, the amount to be paid out each year is not known at the beginning. Therefore, it is the excludable portion that is calculated. This is done by dividing the investment in the contract by the expected return multiple in Table V.[18] Continuing with the same example as above under the fixed payout, $100,000 divided by 20 is $5,000. In our example of a presumed $9,000 payout, at least in the first year, $5,000 of the amount is excludable and $4,000 is includable. Of course, this is simply an example — keep in mind that it is unlikely that fixed payouts and variable payouts would be the same even in the first year. For that reason, it is probable that the difference in the way the two types of payouts are taxed should not be a significant factor in the decision of whether to elect a fixed or a variable payout.

The single life unisex table, Table V, was used in our example because the unisex tables are to be used if the investment in the contract includes investments (premiums) made after June 30, 1986. If there are no investments in the contract after that date, sex-distinct tables are to be used.[19] (One transitional rule allows for an election to use the unisex tables even where there have been no investments in the contract after June 30, 1986. Another provides for an election in some situations to have separate calculations when there have been investments made both before and after the June 30 date.)[20]

How long the annual amount excludable may continue to be excluded is dependent on the annuity starting date, the first day of the first period for which an annuity payment is received.[21] If the annuity starting date is after December 31, 1986, amounts are excluded until the total investment in the contract has been received; after that no amounts are excludable from income and all amounts received are includable.[22] On the other hand, if the annuity starting date was before January 1, 1987, the exclusions continue so that the person receiving the annuity has the same amounts excluded from income throughout the entire payment period not withstanding the fact that the full investment in the contract already has been received.

DEATH OF AN OWNER

The death of an annuity owner has both income and estate tax ramifications. Let us consider the income tax aspects first. When the owner dies before the entire interest in the contract has been paid out, certain distributions must be made. The distributions are a matter of tax policy; they are intended to prevent deferral of income tax on the gains in an annuity contract for years into the future by passing ownership from person to person but not taking taxable distributions.

In order for annuities issued after January 18, 1985 to receive the favorable treatment of deferral of tax on accumulations and spreading of tax on payouts, they must contain two provisions. First, if any owner dies after the annuity starting date but before the entire interest has been distributed, the remaining portion must be distributed at least as rapidly as under the method of distribution being used by the owner at the time of his/her death. Second, if the owner dies before the annuity starting date, the entire interest in the contract must be distributed within the five years following the owner's death.[23] Where there are joint owners of an annuity issued after April 22, 1987, the distribution requirements are applied when the first joint owner dies.[24] When a portion of the owner's interest is to be distributed to a designated beneficiary over the beneficiary's life (or over a period not extending beyond the life expectancy of the beneficiary) and the distribution to the beneficiary begins within one year following the owner's death, that portion is treated as distributed on the day the distribution begins.

When the designated beneficiary is the surviving spouse of the owner, there are special rules. When the spouse, as the designated beneficiary, becomes the new owner, he/she can take the place of the former owner.[25] If the annuity was still in the accumulation stage at the death of the original owner, the spouse can continue in that stage. He/she can add to the annuity if it is a flexible premium type. If the annuity was in the payout stage, the payout would continue according to the terms of the payout provisions. That is, if the provision was for the payout to continue for the remainder of 10 years, for example, then the payments would continue in that fashion. If the annuitant had outlived any guarantee period, payments would cease.

When the owner of an annuity issued after April 22, 1987 is a corporation or other nonnatural person, the primary annuitant is treated as the owner for purposes of applying the distribution rules taking effect at the death of the owner.[26] These distribution requirements are another factor when considering an exchange of an old contract. If a contract issued after January 18, 1985 is received in exchange for one issued before that date, it is considered a new contract and, as a result, subject to the distribution requirements.

The preceding distribution rules apply when the owner dies first or when the annuitant and owner are the same person. Although the majority of nonqualified annuities have the same person as owner and annuitant, sometimes they are different. In our discussion of education funding, there could have been an occasion where, for example, a grandparent could have been the owner while a child or grandchild was the annuitant.

When the annuitant dies first or the annuitant and owner dies, the death benefit as defined in the contract (see the discussion of death benefits in Chapter 7) is paid to the designated beneficiary. If the owner who is not the annuitant dies first, there may be a different death benefit payable. For example, one of the enhanced death benefit provisions may be in effect at the death of the annuitant or annuitant and owner. But merely the accumulated contract values at the death of the owner may be paid when the owner dies before the annuitant.

Planning Tips

Whichever amount is paid at death, the amount is subject to federal income tax essentially the same as when the owner surrenders the contract prior to the annuity starting date. The gain in value over the investment in the contract is taxed as ordinary income in the year it is received. There is no exclusion from income tax as provided to life insurance death benefits. The beneficiary of death benefits does have one way to spread the tax. If the beneficiary elects within 60 days, he/she may apply the benefits under an installment or life income option. In that event, the payments are taxed as the payout provisions applicable to annuity owners described earlier in this chapter.[27]

FEDERAL ESTATE TAX

As we have seen throughout this book, the tax of the most concern with respect to annuities is the income tax. We have discussed deferral of tax during the time values are being accumulated; we have looked at the taxation of withdrawals, including when penalties are applicable; and we have gone into the taxation connected with surrendering the contract or electing to take a fixed or variable payout of the contract values. All of these are important. But there are two other taxes which can be important at times.

The first of these is the federal estate tax. Annuities are property and usually are a part of the estates of people who die while owning them. If someone has been particularly successful at setting aside money and selecting funds which perform well, the contract value of the annuity will be substantial. It can add significantly to the other assets in the person's estate — the personal residence, and any other real property, the values in qualified retirement plans, life insurance owned, other savings and investments, and, perhaps, an interest in a small business.

People often are complacent about the estate tax since it seems to take a significant amount of assets for an estate tax to be payable. Some of the complacence is understandable. Unless there are assets of more than $600,000, after deduction of debts and funeral expenses, there is no tax because of the unified credit unless some of the credit had been used earlier to avoid gift tax. An estate has a credit of $192,800, the tax that would be due on $600,000 of assets. This amount is scheduled to increase each year until it reaches $1,000,000 in the year 2006. A married individual can leave all of the assets to his/her spouse and have no taxable estate because of the unlimited marital deduction.

But for many people, this would be short-sighted. If a person leaves all assets to a spouse, the spouse's estate will be subject to a sizable tax at time of death. If the assets left continue to appreciate, as all hope they will, the tax is that much more before the remaining assets are available to children. It would have been better for the first spouse to leave at least the amount covered by the unified credit to children with income going to the surviving spouse while he/she was alive. Then, the second estate would have been smaller by the unified credit covered amount. In these days of high divorce rates, it may be short-sighted to rely too much on the marital deduction. In fact, estate planning today often involves two or more families and must be done with care and deftness.

Reminder

Another point to remember is what the estate tax rate is likely to be when it is assessed. Although the rates go from 18 percent to 55 percent (with a 5 percent add on for amounts between $10,000,000 and $21,040,000), few estates will be taxed at the lowest rates. That is because of the way the calculation is made. The tax is calculated and then the unified credit is subtracted. This means that where the full unified credit is available, the first amount taxed above $600,000 is at 37 percent. For all intents and purposes, the minimum rate is 37 percent in these cases. That makes the stakes high indeed. Anyone close to having an estate tax liability needs to engage in estate planning which will minimize, to the extent practicable, the estate tax to be paid by both spouses' estates.

A variable annuity in the accumulation phase will have a death benefit payable to a beneficiary, as discussed in Chapter 7 and earlier in this chapter. When the owner and annuitant dies, the value of the annuity, presumably the death benefit, is included in his/her estate.[28] When an annuitant who is not the owner dies, there is a payment to a beneficiary but the annuitant had no interest to be included in his/her estate. When an owner who is not the annuitant dies, the value of the annuity is what is referred to as replacement cost, the amount that it would cost to purchase a comparable annuity contract at the time of the owner's death.[29]

When an annuity is in the payout phase, the death benefit in the contract usually no longer is applicable. And the remaining value of the annuity depends on what type of payout provisions are operating. If a life income with no term certain or refund is in effect, nothing would be paid to a beneficiary and, for that reason, nothing would be includable in the owner's estate. Where there is a fixed period or fixed amount option selected, and all payments have not yet been received, the value of the unpaid installments would be includable. Similarly, where there is a life income with a period certain in effect, and the annuitant-owner dies before the period certain has run, the value of the unpaid installments is includable.[30] The value to be included is the present value of the payments; that is, interest that would have been earned over the remaining period is subtracted from the total of the remaining installments.

When two people use a joint and survivor annuity payout, and one of the two dies, the remaining value to be paid out is the amount, if any, that would be includable. The remaining value is the replacement value, the amount the same insurance company would charge for a single life annuity at the age of the surviving joint annuitant at the time of the death of the first.[31] However, two factors affect how much and whether that is actually includable. If both people had contributed to the purchase of the annuity, only that amount purchased by the decedent would be includable.[32] Also, if the two are a married couple, the remaining value is eligible for the marital deduction.[33] This would mean that none of the value is includable in the taxable estate of the decedent. If the two are not a married couple, the marital deduction is not available. Some joint and survivor payouts also have term certain provisions, applicable when both annuitants die before a period of years has run. In that case, any remaining value would be includable in the estate of the second to die.

Survivor benefits attributable to employer contributions in qualified retirement plans have been treated in a variety of ways for federal estate tax purposes over the years. Benefits paid to the estates of decedents dying after 1953 and before 1983 had a complete exclusion from estate tax. More recently, there was an exclusion of up to $100,000 for the estates of decedents dying after 1982 and before 1985. However, estates of decedents dying after 1984 have no exclusion.[34] Note that under certain circumstances the pre-1984 exclusion may have been preserved. There also are no exclusions for other types of plans such as IRAs and TSAs although the effective dates of some of the changes are somewhat different.

FEDERAL GIFT TAX

Making gifts during lifetime is an often used estate planning technique. Most property given away no longer will be in the estate of someone who dies after the gifts are made. But someone cannot simply give away everything just before death, thereby avoiding estate tax, because there will be gift tax to pay when much of the property is given away.

Moreover, the federal estate and gift taxes are a unified system. Estate tax and gift tax rates are the same. Lifetime gifts subject to the gift tax are taken into account when determining the size of the taxable estate of a decedent. In effect, if gifts have been made, and all or a portion of the unified credit applied so that less or no tax was paid at the time of the gifts, that portion of the unified credit is used up and not available to reduce the estate tax. Recall that the unified credit is $192,800, enough to offset paying gift or estate tax on $600,000 of property (and more in years after 1997). Some people will elect not to apply the unified credit when they make gifts so that it can be retained for use when the estate tax is paid. In such cases, the property given away is out of the eventual estate and so is the cash used to pay the gift tax.

Planning Tips

Outright gifts to other persons are subject to an annual exclusion of $10,000 per recipient. A parent could give $10,000 to each of his/her five adult children; if both parents agree to "split" a gift, the amount can be doubled without gift tax,[35] a total of $20,000 per child per year. The amount of this annual exclusion will be indexed in future years.

For parents in normal health, this is an extremely valuable estate planning technique. Only gifts of a present interest are eligible for the annual exclusion. A present interest gift is one which the recipient can have immediate enjoyment and control. In contrast, a gift of a future interest is one where the right to use the property is at some point in the future. Gifts of a future interest usually are those given in trust with restrictions being placed on immediate control and enjoyment. Outright gifts are of a present interest.

The gift tax also has an unlimited marital deduction. That is, gifts made to a spouse are deducted from the gifts made for a year and, therefore, not subject to the gift tax.[36] As a result, an estate owner does not have to be overly concerned about transfers of property to a spouse where the transfers may be seen to be gifts. In fact, they may be gifts but not subject to tax because of the marital deduction.

Gifts to a qualified charity generally are deducted from other gifts made for the year and not subject to gift tax. Several types of charitable trusts are discussed in Chapter 11. Generally, no charitable deduction from the gift tax is allowed for the lead interest (in a charitable lead trust) unless the payments to the charity are made as a guaranteed annuity or as a fixed percentage of the property's fair market value. Further, no charitable deduction is available for a remainder interest in a trust unless the trust qualifies as either a charitable remainder annuity trust, a charitable remainder unitrust, or a pooled income fund.[37] A gift tax charitable deduction is allowed for a charitable gift annuity (where the gift is made in exchange for an annuity to be paid by the charity) if the value of the gift exceeds the value of the annuity, and the annuity is payable out of the general funds of the charity.[38]

ANNUITIES AS GIFTS

We have discussed the gift tax and need now to look at when a gift can arise with respect to the purchase of an annuity. When a parent or grandparent pays the premium on an annuity owned by a child or grandchild, a gift of the premium has been made.[39] So long as the premium is $10,000 or less (as indexed), the annual exclusion applies. The gift of the premium on a single premium annuity probably would exceed the exclusion, however. If the donor wants not to involve either paying a gift tax or applying a portion of the unified credit, the arrangement should be structured to stay within the annual exclusion, noting that the annual amount that may be excluded is $20,000 when a split gift with the donor's spouse is possible.

When a person wants to enter into a joint and survivor annuity with someone else, there is the potential for a gift, presuming that the first person is the source of all or most of the premiums to be paid. If the person retains the right to change the other joint annuitant, the gift will not have been completed. But that is not the usual situation with joint and survivor annuities. When it is an immediate annuity, it usually is issued on the basis of the two people involved and, therefore, is irrevocable. When it is a deferred annuity, both owners usually have rights jointly. If the two joint annuitants are married to each other, the fact that there may be a gift is not important because of the unlimited marital deduction. If the two are not married, then there is likely to be a gift at the time the person who provides the money for premiums no longer retains the right to make changes without the consent of the other person.[40]

When there is a single life annuity with a period certain guarantee, a gift will arise if the beneficiary is named irrevocably. That is the case in spite of the fact that the beneficiary may not ever receive anything because the annuitant lives beyond the period certain. Obviously, this can be avoided by leaving the beneficiary designation revocable, which is the usual practice.

Caution

The owner of an annuity can make an assignment of the contract; this is a gift and will be subject to gift tax[41] unless the value of the contract is within the annual exclusion or the assignee is the spouse of the owner. Perhaps more serious is the income tax consideration if the annuity was issued after April 22, 1987. The donor of the gift of the annuity is treated as having received the contract value less the investment in the contract,[42] the same income tax result as if the person had surrendered the contract. This goes beyond the gift tax considerations. About the only positive impact of such a situation is the fact that the donee of the gift will receive a higher income tax basis in the contract than he/she would have received if this special provision did not apply. This means that if the new owner of the contract decides to surrender it later, there will be less gain since the original owner had already been subject to tax for the gain that had occurred prior to the gift.

When an annuity is given to another person as a gift, the value of the gift depends on several factors. If it is given immediately after the purchase, the value is the price paid by the donor; that is, it is the amount of the premium paid, single premium, for example. If the gift is made after some increases in values have occurred, the gift value is the replacement cost, that is, the premium required to purchase a similar contract from the same issuer. When one person purchases a joint and survivor annuity naming himself/herself and another person as joint annuitants, the gift value is the cost of the joint and survivor contract, less the cost of a single life annuity for the person who supplied the cash for the purchase. Note that if the two people are spouses, any gift is subject to the unlimited marital deduction.[43]

PLANNING CONSIDERATIONS

As we have seen, there are numerous considerations involving who owns an annuity, who the annuitant or annuitants are, and who the beneficiary is. These considerations can involve income and gift taxes and can impact the estate tax that eventually may be payable. Most attention is given to income tax — the deductibility of current contributions to IRAs, SEPs, TSAs, and qualified retirement plans; the deferral of current income tax while the values in the contract accumulate; when and how much income tax may be payable when withdrawals from the contract are made. In addition, most people have at least a notion that income tax can be spread out when a life income option, fixed or variable, is elected later in life. There usually is at least some recognition that annuities owned may be includable in estates for estate tax purposes. Relatively little attention is given to the gift tax aspects of transferring annuities or naming beneficiaries.

Yet, it is important to avoid gift tax involvement where possible. For example, when an annuity owner names a child as beneficiary for sentimental reasons, there will be a gift tax consideration should the owner die during the accumulation period. The situation could have been avoided by naming the spouse as beneficiary. More than that, if the spouse had been named beneficiary, that spouse might have benefited a great deal by being able to continue the annuity and the income tax deferral of accumulations of values inside the annuity.

There are a number of instances where similar considerations could enter the picture. The important point is that a valuable service that can be given to someone who purchases an annuity is to coordinate ownership and beneficiary designations with other financial and estate planning provisions. There are so many choices to be made at the beginning (not the least of which is the selection of variable accounts) but these ownership and beneficiary considerations should be given due weight.

CHAPTER FOOTNOTES

1. See generally IRC Section 72.

2. IRC Section 72(u).

3. IRC Section 72(u)(2).

4. IRC Section 72(u)(i).

5. IRC Sections 72(e)(2), 72(e)(3).

6. IRC Section 72(e)(5)(B).

7. Rev. Rul. 85-159, 1985-2 CB 29.

8. *Ibid.*

9. IRC Section 72(q)(2).

10. IRC Section 72(e)(11).

11. Reg. §1.1035-1.

12. Rev. Rul. 68-235, 1968-1 CB 360; Rev. Rul. 72-358, 1972-2 CB 473.

13. Reg. §1.1031(b)-1(a).

14. Reg. §1.1031(b)-1(c).

15. IRC Section 72(e)(5)(E).

16. IRC Section 165.

17. IRC Section 72(b)(1).

18. Reg. §1.72-2(b)(3).

19. Reg. §§1.72-5(a), 1.72-5(b).

20. Reg. §1.72-9.

21. IRC Section 72(c)(4); Reg. §1.72-4(b).

22. IRC Section 72(b)(2).

23. IRC Section 72(s)(1).

24. Tax Reform Act of 1986, P.L. 99-514, Section 1826(b)(2).

25. IRC Section 72(s)(3).

26. IRC Section 72(s)(6).

27. IRC Section 73(h); Reg. §§1.72-11(a), 1.72-11(e).

28. IRC Sections 2033, 2039; Reg. §20.2039-1(d).

29. IRC Section 2031; Reg. Section 20.2031-1(b).

30. IRC Sections 2033, 2039.

31. Reg. §20.2031-8.

32. IRC Section 2039.

33. IRC Section 2056.

34. IRC Section 2039, as prior to and altered by The Tax Equity and Fiscal Responsibility Act of 1982, P.L. 97-248, and The Deficit Reduction Act of 1984, P.L. 98-369. Note that under certain circumstances the pre-1984 exclusion may have been preserved.

35. IRC Section 2513.

36. IRC Section 2523(a).

37. IRC Section 2522.

38. IRC Section 2522(a); Rev. Rul. 80-281, 1980-2 CB 282.

39. Reg. §25.2511-1(h)(8).

40. Rev. Rul. 55-388, 1955-1 CB 233; Reg. §25.2511-1.

41. Reg. §25.2511-1(h)(8).

42. IRC Section 72(e)(4)(C).

43. Reg. §25.2512-6.

APPENDIX

The following lists, charts, and graphs provide useful information about variable annuity product features and sales results. This material is reproduced from *The Variable Annuity Research & Data Service (VARDS) Report*. Readers interested in additional information of this sort may contact Mr. R. H. Carey, Editor and Publisher, at Financial Planning Resources, Inc., 4343 Shallowford Road, Suite B-6, Marietta, Georgia, 30062, (770) 998-5186.

Figure 1

The VARDS Report
Average Annual Historic Quarterly Variable Annuity Sales

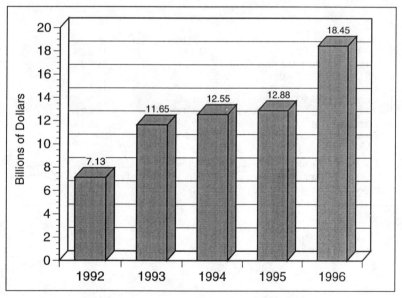

The VARDS Report, Special Report, Year-End (12/31/96) Sales and Asset Survey. Copyright 1997 Financial Planning Resources, Inc. Data is representative of the VARDS universe only. No estimations have been made. Sales are reported on an individual product by product basis. Reproduced by permission.

Figure 2

The VARDS Report - Variable Annuity Assets By Investment Objective
As of September 30, 1997

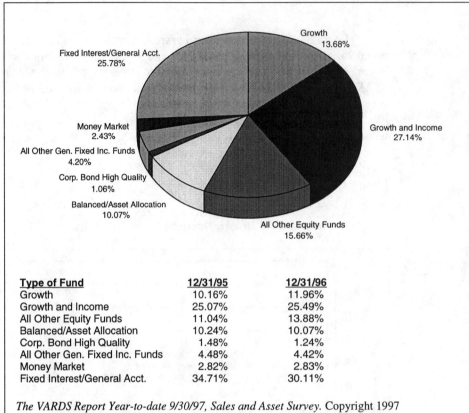

Type of Fund	12/31/95	12/31/96
Growth	10.16%	11.96%
Growth and Income	25.07%	25.49%
All Other Equity Funds	11.04%	13.88%
Balanced/Asset Allocation	10.24%	10.07%
Corp. Bond High Quality	1.48%	1.24%
All Other Gen. Fixed Inc. Funds	4.48%	4.42%
Money Market	2.82%	2.83%
Fixed Interest/General Acct.	34.71%	30.11%

The VARDS Report Year-to-date 9/30/97, Sales and Asset Survey. Copyright 1997
Financial Planning Resources, Inc. Data is representative of the VARDS universe only.
Reproduced by permission.

Figure 3

VARDS MARKET AVERAGES Performance Through October 31, 1997 Ranked by YTD						
CATEGORY	YTD	1 Yr Avg	2 Yr Avg	3 Yr Avg	4 Yr Avg	5 Yr Avg
Growth and Income Funds	20.31%	26.52%	23.46%	22.45%	16.98%	16.62%
Growth Funds	19.91%	24.58%	20.20%	22.04%	16.37%	17.19%
Equity-Income Funds	19.64%	25.05%	21.36%	20.73%	16.56%	17.50%
Small Company Funds	16.46%	20.55%	17.38%	20.33%	15.40%	17.86%
All Equity Funds	15.16%	20.07%	18.16%	17.84%	13.97%	15.69%
Aggressive Growth Funds	14.56%	16.49%	17.25%	19.18%	14.53%	17.92%
All Balanced Funds	13.84%	17.53%	15.22%	15.00%	10.65%	11.47%
Specialty Funds	11.65%	18.60%	18.43%	16.18%	11.36%	13.80%
Corporate Bond High Yield Funds	10.65%	13.77%	12.76%	13.05%	9.41%	11.19%
Government Bond - Treasury Funds	7.85%	8.47%	5.73%	11.32%	4.82%	8.64%
All Fixed - Income/Bond Funds	6.67%	8.07%	7.32%	9.15%	5.60%	7.02%
Government Bond Mtg-Backed Funds	6.57%	7.34%	5.97%	8.35%	4.83%	6.72%
Corporate Bond General Funds	6.50%	7.65%	6.56%	8.73%	5.07%	6.56%
Corporate Bond High Quality Funds	6.37%	7.01%	5.62%	7.99%	4.53%	5.85%
Government Bond General Funds	5.98%	6.52%	5.03%	7.34%	3.93%	5.05%
International Stock Funds	4.23%	8.89%	10.67%	7.00%	7.87%	11.77%
All Money Market Funds	3.22%	3.86%	3.84%	3.97%	3.52%	3.12%
International Bond Funds	1.54%	2.99%	6.03%	6.75%	4.09%	5.16%

The VARDS Report, October 1997 Analysis. Reproduced by permission.

Figure 4

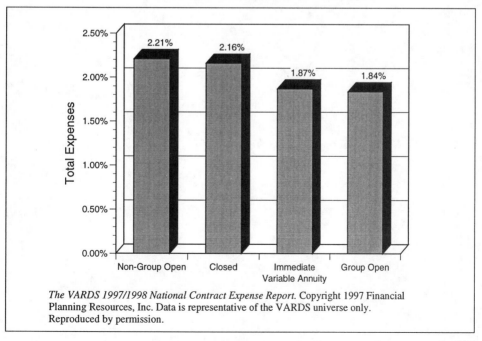

The VARDS Report
1997/1998 Average National Expense Level (all types)

The VARDS 1997/1998 National Contract Expense Report. Copyright 1997 Financial Planning Resources, Inc. Data is representative of the VARDS universe only. Reproduced by permission.

Figure 5

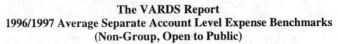

The VARDS Report
1996/1997 Average Separate Account Level Expense Benchmarks
(Non-Group, Open to Public)

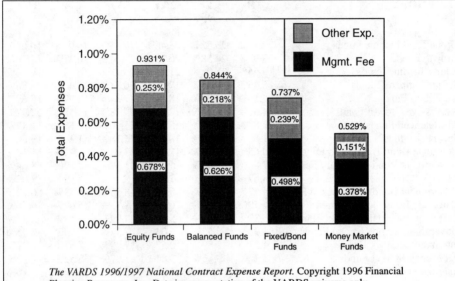

The VARDS 1996/1997 National Contract Expense Report. Copyright 1996 Financial
Planning Resources, Inc. Data is representative of the VARDS universe only.
Reproduced by permission.

INDEX

T

U

V

W